How to work as a
FREELANCE
JOURNALIST

Visit our How To website at www.howto.co.uk

At **www.howto.co.uk** you can engage in conversation with our authors – all of whom have 'been there and done that' in their specialist fields. You can get access to special offers and additional content but most importantly you will be able to engage with, and become a part of, a wide and growing community of people just like yourself.

At **www.howto.co.uk** you'll be able to talk and share tips with people who have similar interests and are facing similar challenges in their lives. People who, just like you, have the desire to change their lives for the better – be it through moving to a new country, starting a new business, growing their own vegetables, or writing a novel.

At **www.howto.co.uk** you'll find the support and encouragement you need to help make your aspirations a reality.

You can go direct to www.how-to-work-as-a-freelance-journalist.co.uk which is part of the main How To site.

How To Books strives to present authentic, inspiring, practical information in their books. Now, when you buy a title from **How To Books**, you get even more than just words on a page.

How to work as a
FREELANCE
JOURNALIST

Marc Leverton

howtobooks

Published by How To Books Ltd
Spring Hill House, Spring Hill Road
Begbroke, Oxford OX5 1RX
Tel: (01865) 375794. Fax: (01865) 379162
info@howtobooks.co.uk
www.howtobooks.co.uk

How To Books greatly reduce the carbon footprint of their books by
sourcing their typesetting and printing in the UK.

British Library Cataloguing in Publication Data
A catalogue record for this book is available from the British Library

ISBN: 978 1 84528 395 7

Produced for How To Books by Deer Park Productions, Tavistock
Typeset by Pantek Arts Ltd, Maidstone, Kent
Printed and bound by Bell & Bain Ltd, Glasgow

Contents

Introduction

WHAT IS A FREELANCE JOURNALIST?

A journalist is a person who writes reports and articles for magazines and newspapers. Someone who is freelance is someone who gets paid for an agreed piece of work on a self-employed basis. A freelance journalist therefore works for a variety of media companies producing written content to suit each publication. It is so simple to explain; I only wish it was so easy to achieve.

I had to resist the temptation of writing an introduction to working as a freelance journalist so off-putting and so full of scare stories that any sensible person would stop reading right here and reconsider trying their hand at the world's 'second oldest profession'. The truth is that, despite everything, journalism remains a great job. One of the best. If you can get the work.

Working as a journalist allows you to follow your curiosity and interests and to ask questions about things that under normal circumstances would get a door slammed in your face. It is often stated that being a journalist 'gives you the keys to the city' in the sense that you have a pass to speak to all strands of society. It has been my pleasure to interview the homeless, MPs, celebrities, drug users, authors, members of the council, musicians, a strongwoman, business people, a laughter therapist and a magician.

ABOUT THIS BOOK

The first half of this guide will introduce you to the various forms that journalism takes. Plus other information that makes up the least that an editor would expect a budding journalist to know, and a bit more that they might not.

The second half will introduce you to the business of freelancing. This will hopefully be useful for beginners and for the seasoned journalist alike, as many established journalists in staff positions are still smarting from being forced into freelancing by the recent waves of redundancies made to local newspapers.

In the danger of sounding like I am making an acceptance speech, I would very much like to publicly thank all of the journalists who have contributed their time and energy and put up with me poking about in their professional lives. This advice from the many contributors will prove invaluable and I hope will make your career path less painful than ours.

The reason I have structured the first half of the book into the different types of journalism that you might find in an average magazine or newspaper is to help you develop your own niche. Developing a niche isn't essential but can give you a considerable advantage.

If you are approaching this book without having done any writing before then learning to write in as many different styles as possible and trying the exercises will help develop your 'writing muscles' and increase confidence in your own abilities.

This is the book I wish I had been able to read when I was starting out as a freelance journalist. I remember trying to find books about journalism basics myself, which proved problematic –

most journalists tended to write books at the end of their careers. A collection of amusing anecdotes from the halcyon days of journalism, they also tended to be 'top-end' journalists and not very useful to a jobbing hack based outside London.

I also found a couple of inspirational 'Quit the grind and write your way to freedom' type of books, which may provide a quick boost. A sugar rush. Before long you are back to holding your head in your hands questioning why the hell you decided to enter a trade where people are being laid off at an alarming rate.

If you are lucky enough to have a clear direction of where you want to go within journalism I would still urge you to read the other areas in Part One. As journalism becomes a tougher industry to make a living in, you will need to continue to improve your skills, expand your horizons and develop more niches.

DEVELOPING MEDIA LITERACY

Another good reason to read through the different styles of journalism is to help digest the vast amount of information that is pumped out at us every day. The 'consumption' of media is so great that we are in danger of becoming obese. It is easy to feel overwhelmed by all this information, and disseminating true facts from opinions, gossip and educated comment is increasingly difficult. Reading a magazine or newspaper can be a less arduous task if you can separate the wheat from the chaff.

Above all, I hope that this is a practical guide that helps you to find the course that you need to take to enter a tough but rewarding profession.

FINDINGS ABOUT THE INDUSTRY

The interviews with journalists in this book also serve as a snapshot of the industry in 2009/10. Almost everyone interviewed says that their jobs are great, but express some concern about recent changes in the industry that have devalued the profession – namely pay freezes and redundancies. Let's hope that the next few years prove to be a turning point for the fortunes of journalists, freelance and staff.

Perhaps the greatest revelation is that many freelance journalists are working part-time, mostly out of necessity as work is hard to find. Many also supplement their work with some other job, which pays better than journalism. In my case, this is teaching. But for others it is working in PR, television, unions, copywriting. The other scenario, as Brendan Foley points out in the interview in Chapter 6, is that part-time journalists can be supplemented by a partner's wages.

ABOUT ME

I don't write about myself here for egotistical reasons, but rather to demonstrate that it is possible to make several false starts, some bad decisions, bury your head in the sand for a bit, change careers, make slow progress and then finally arrive at your goal. Oh well, better late than never.

I came to journalism the long way round; I made several attempts from an early age. I had my first piece published aged 16 in a fanzine, then some more in a student magazine in my early twenties, and then one or two more in my late twenties for a local paper. I suffered from a delusion that someone somewhere would notice my writing and offer me a job. They didn't of course, and I continued to work unhappily in various jobs wondering what the hell I was going to do with my life.

Working in advertising sales for *The Big Issue* I started to see first hand how journalists and freelancers plied their trade. Working in sales for a few years also thickened my skin, which I needed. I worked up the food chain at the magazine and slowly became more and more involved in the editorial side, working a lot in my own time. Eventually becoming Publisher, which meant managing the magazine's advertising and editorial departments.

I had always wanted to work for myself and being freelance was a chance for me to do this and to finally concentrate completely on my journalism skills. Working freelance has been an additional challenge, and is not one to be taken lightly.

I have been a professional journalist (I define 'professional' as getting paid for my work) since 2005. I realise I am just a few years down the track, and not one of the seasoned hacks that I mentioned have also written books. I think this is to my advantage for writing a 'beginner's guide' as I can remember what it is like starting out.

I have written for a regional magazine, local 'what's on' magazines, online magazines, a national newspaper, trade magazines and business magazines. In that order, I built up from writing gig reviews and CD reviews free of charge to writing features and getting paid for them.

I have had several niches in this time. I began by writing about music for fanzines and the student magazine. I wrote and read the news for the student radio station. At *The Big Issue* I wrote gig reviews first before moving on to small interview pieces and then full features. For other magazines I used my knowledge of homelessness and the social sector to write about volunteering, drugs, prisons and charities. Along the way I have also written about travel, business, gadgets, sport and food.

Nowadays I also work as a teacher at Bath Spa University, helping undergraduates to navigate their own paths through the media and creative industries jungle. I hope this book also guides you through that same jungle.

Part One

Learning to write as a journalist

1

Tools of the trade

When I worked at *The Big Issue*, about once a week the phone would ring:

'Hello, I have written a story about a homeless man.'

'I'm sorry we don't publish short stories.'

'Ha. Yes you do, I am looking at one right now.'

'Ah, yes. Well, that was a story donated by Will Self. Perhaps I should have said we don't publish stories by unknown authors.'

'I am very well known in Dorset.'

'Sorry.'

'But it is about a homeless man.'

'Sorry, not one for us. Good luck.'

The first section of this book will introduce you to the tools of the trade. Before you start writing you need to understand something about who you are writing for, so the next chapter on readership is absolutely required reading. Read that, and you have my permission to skip, skim and cherry pick to your heart's content.

WRITING ABILITY – NATURE OR NURTURE?

It goes without saying that a freelance journalist is going to need to write. Contrary to popular myths, sometimes perpetuated by writers themselves, writing isn't a god-given gift. Every child needs to learn how to read and write, and parents will tell you that kids take to these skills with varying degrees of enthusiasm. But that doesn't mean that someone can't learn and develop the techniques and skills that make them a better writer.

Journalism is a trade and writing is a craft. To become a journalist you will need to learn techniques; and to become a master craftsperson you will need to develop your skills over a period of time. But all craftspeople need to start somewhere and the techniques explained here will give you the basis you need; the rest is down to your application of those skills.

When I became a full-time freelance journalist I met up with an old editor friend of mine. I told him that I was worried that I just wasn't going to be a good enough writer. 'Don't worry,' he said, 'writing comes in increments, you will become better and better the more you do.' He was right. Another friend who is a very good guitarist said that learning the guitar is the same. You don't pick up a guitar and expect to play it straight away – you learn a few chords and progress. Remember that some of the best songs ever written have only three chords.

If you are still wondering if you are properly 'tooled up' to become a freelance journalist, read the section called 'The "Am I up to it?" skills test' in Chapter 17. It might just assure you that it is a rare beast that can claim to know everything about everything.

I have chosen to structure the first half of the book as a series of journalistic styles for good reason. Any editor will be more than familiar with the freelance journalist sending in ideas which may be great but which just don't *fit*. Reading your chosen magazine or newspaper regularly will help you to identify potential areas that might fit with your ideas.

So how do we go about creating pieces that fit? Well, let's go through the sections that most newpapers and magazines include and you can start to work out what kind of stuff you might like to produce.

ESSENTIAL TOOLKIT

But before we do, let's return to our essential toolkit. Just as a painter needs a brush, a journalist can't be without their armoury of questions.

Who, what, why, where, when and how?

If you remember nothing else, remember these. They are essential to the job of journalism but aren't all you need to get started: you also need to have a good knowledge of your audience or the 'readership' as it is often referred to. Your audience dictates so much of what you will write; people buy their magazines and newspapers because they know what to expect from them. It is only the odd journalist who becomes known and has their name and a photo emblazoned across a page.

The following will help you to identify what you are going to write and for whom.

HARDWARE

Other tools of the trade that you will need are a bit more predictable. If you don't know shorthand (which I don't) then you are going to need something to record interviews with. You also need a computer for typing up your work and access to email and the internet to contact editors and submit work.

The internet has had a huge impact on journalism and journalists' work – information is available at the touch of a button and has taken a lot of the old legwork out of the job.

For recording interviews nowadays I just use the record function on my mobile phone; this especially is ideal for phone interviews. I also find that there is something less obtrusive about a mobile these days. I used to use an MP3 player with a small microphone, but people don't like talking into microphones. Leaving a phone in front of someone while you talk hardly goes noticed and interviews will be a lot more natural as a result.

So I have recorded my interview. I now need to go back to the office to type it up. This is called transcription – I used to be very slow at this and spend a lot of time transcribing the whole interview. Over time I have been able to just listen through and hear what sounds like a good quote. Typing ability is a great help here.

So as you can see the skills are straightforward enough, and the tools needed for the job are within the reach of most people. Think of journalism as a craft; it is easy to nail a few bits of wood together but that doesn't make you a carpenter. And so it is with journalism. We will start with the easier end of the trade and progress to some of the more complicated elements. Go at your own pace and work through the writing exercises included throughout Part One, taking as much time as you need.

2

Who is the audience?

Before we start writing, whatever it might be, we need to know who it is for. This is so that we can write in a manner that is appropriate for the audience we are addressing. It is no good using a casual, relaxed tone for an up-market business magazine for example. In publishing, the audience is referred to as the 'readership'.

RESEARCHING A PUBLICATION

A lot can be picked up from simply reading the publication you want to research, and this is often the first piece of advice editors give to prospective freelancers. By reading through a publication we can find out:

■ What is its tone? Is it serious and informed, or relaxed and witty?

■ What do they publish? If it is mostly features and news it is unlikely they will take your opinion piece.

■ Are you suggesting something that fits within the current format of the publication? Note sections, word lengths and 'by lines' (see Appendix 1, Jargon Buster).

■ Is there a list of staff and contributors in the 'flannel panel' (see Appendix 1, Jargon Buster)? This list and 'by lines' are signs that they do take freelance contributions.

An editor will have a very good idea of the target readership of their publication. They will know their age, their interests, where they live and what kinds of things they will want to see in their favourite magazine or newspaper. You might not be able to ask the editor for all this information but it might be available on their website through the advertising department.

READER PROFILE – MEDIA PACK

Advertising departments produce media packs for prospective advertisers. They are full of the kind of demographical information that marketing managers need to know in order to justify spending their advertising budget. Essentially they look to match the demographic of their target audience with a publication that does the same.

If I were the marketing manager of a London-based university, for example, I would be looking for prospective students aged 16–18; plus I might also know that students come from all over the UK and abroad as well (mainly from China). So I would take out adverts in some national youth-based magazines such as *NME* and *Seventeen* but also the *Shanghai Post* as this is what the parents of my Chinese students are most likely to read.

Most publications have a media pack online which details the demographics of their readership.

How else can a media pack help the freelance journalist?

1. It helps you pitch suitable ideas. Surprisingly this is the most common error of the freelance journalist. Although taking an idea to more than one editor is a good idea, the editor will quickly be able to tell if you have never read their publication.

2. It can generate ideas. One magazine I have written for is *Real Travel*. Their readership is mostly aged 18–30 but there is a percentage of readers aged 55–65 with a high disposable income. So it might work in my favour to think of something that suits the older group – 'White water rafting for the over 50s', for example.

3. Publications often like to publish something inspired by their advertising as it guarantees their advertising income. If you noticed adverts for a new product or service it might trigger an idea such as 'Are these new style of walking shoes any good?'

If a publication doesn't have a media pack online, or if you are not online yourself, look at the adverts in it and see if there are any further clues to the readership's age and interests that can't be ascertained from the articles. If there are adverts for cars, it is probably likely that the readers have a good amount of disposable income. So is your idea about budget travel in Asia best suited to them? Perhaps something a bit more up-market would be appropriate?

The Oldie magazine – an example

- 86% ABC1

Average income: £30,095 (but a lot would not answer the question!)

60% have stocks and shares

Internet usage
- 74% of Oldies own a computer and regularly surf the internet
- 53% have a broadband connection
- Over 88% purchase books and over 66% book travel online

So *Oldie* readers are used to buying products online.

Charitable
- An incredible 73% of *Oldie* readers give to charities three or more times a year.

Our charity advertisers such as Christian Aid, RNLI and Practical Action get a great response.

Travel
- Most *Oldie* readers take two or more holidays abroad a year
- 67% of Oldies travel by air and 15% regularly go on cruises

Educated
- Oldies read quality dailies, with 36% taking the *Daily Telegraph*
- 87% of our readers cite reading as their favourite pastime
- 42% regularly visit art galleries and 41% regularly attend concerts

Oldies enjoy a drink
- 34% of Oldies regularly drink vintage wine and 42% drink malt whisky

A sense of fun
- 73% of Oldies said they liked the cartoons the most

Our cartoons set us apart: no other magazine has as many quality cartoons every month that entertain and make you smile.

So now I have all of this information I can start thinking of ideas that might appeal. For example, I might write about a charity that promotes education abroad, taking stocks and shares in companies that produce alcohol, perhaps the future of reading and whether eReaders are going to catch on.

Some of these ideas might have already been written about, of course, which is why editors always prefer it if you regularly read their publication. It isn't possible to read every publication every time it is published, but sometimes you can search their websites to see if your ideas have been covered before.

3

Writing reviews

Definition

A review is a shorter piece of writing that gives the reader an overview of a new thing. That 'thing' is often cultural such as a CD, DVD, book, game, gig, theatre or comedy show, but it could also be something like a gadget or a car.

Reviewers are often described as 'critics' and reviews can range from highbrow critical assessments made by respected commentators with a specialist subject (such as *The Times*'s restaurant critic AA Gil) to a general overview that keeps the reader up to date with what is going on in the world. Each has their place and writing a good review starts with knowing what is required before you begin writing.

STARTING POINT

Reviews are traditionally a starting point for any budding journalist. They are short for a start so the chances of going wrong are much less. But also they fill regular space in a magazine and make it seem relevant with its finger on the pulse. Readers of magazines are often enthusiasts who buy them to keep informed about the latest music, books or films, so reviews maintain sales to those readers and keep potential advertisers happy.

It is common for magazines to farm out reviews to people looking for work experience and students without costing the paper anything. The writer bags a free CD, DVD or book if they are lucky and they also get their name in print. Everyone is happy.

Well, it is rare that 'everyone is happy' – you have a few other briefs to hit first.

WRITING FOR AN AUDIENCE

As already mentioned, every publication has a different audience and that audience will have specific expectations of their favourite magazine. Slate a reader's favourite band and next week's letters' page might read like this:

> 'Calling Metallica "a bunch of ageing turds" is the kind of comment I'd expect to read in *Viz* magazine. Rest assured, as editor of the Metallica website I will make sure that our 100,000 million members will be boycotting your magazine for the rest of time.'
>
> Angry editor, L.A.

So read the magazine to get an idea of the style of review the publication publishes. Or better still, ask the editor, who will probably say 'read the magazine' anyway but they will be glad you asked.

The essence of reviewing is how honest should you be? Assuming the publication is mainstream media with a general audience, you are looking to offer rational thought about a piece of work's strengths and weaknesses before informing the reader whether they should part with their hard-earned cash to invest in the latest CD, DVD, movie, etc. If you hate Madonna and all that she stands for, chances are you aren't going to give her a balanced review and it is probably worth leaving it for someone else.

Phil Sutcliffe suggests, in the interview in Chapter 10, that one of the cardinal sins new journalists make is starting with themselves, i.e. 'I think this band sucks'. It is obvious that a review can never be entirely objective but the journalist should at least strive for some objectivity in their writing. This is what separates a 'critic' from a 'ranter'. So, 'I think this band has seen better days. Their last album sold appallingly and they are now back playing in the smaller venues that they may have thought they had see the last of' offers a more balanced and fair assessment of a band's career.

Some online sites and more specialised publications may allow a more scathing review, to which there isn't much to say. Just go for it, and try and be witty and funny at the same time because just plain angry is a bit weird and a bit scary and says more about you than it does about the subject you are writing about.

Review writing exercise

Write a 100–200 word review for a mainstream audience. Think of your local paper and imagine you are writing for a mixed audience of grandparents, bus drivers and young people.

Your piece is for the arts section of the paper, so you could write a review of a gig you have seen recently, or a film, theatre performance, DVD or even a television programme.

Try to avoid clichés such as, 'He sang in the great way that he can and the atmosphere was electric'. Think about why it was special. What type of people made up the audience? We don't just want a list of songs played.

I also suggest you grab a piece of a paper and do this without thinking about it too much. It would be very easy to think 'I'll do it later', but will you really? Do it now, and give yourself 10–15 minutes to complete a rough draft.

Don't worry if you don't think it is perfect – one of the secrets of writing is that much of the work is in the re-write. It is rare that a first draft of anything will be the finished article. You can go back later and polish it – for now just get something down that you can work on later.

EXPAND YOUR HORIZONS

After the above exercise you could go on to write a series of reviews. The more material you have to show someone, the better. Also the more you practice, the better you will become. The process of review writing also makes you work harder when you listen, see or experience things, and this will help you appreciate culture in a new way.

If you have a favourite magazine or website, imagine you are writing reviews for that publication. Once you have a collection of about ten review, you could try sending them to that magazine and see if you get any feedback.

KILL YOUR DARLINGS

The other reason I suggest writing a collection of reviews is that it will allow you to start to identify any bad habits you fall into. On creative writing courses they call this 'Killing your darlings'.

An example might be something like starting a review with 'On a first listen, this sounds like any other contemporary band but … blah, blah, blah'. This isn't a bad opening in itself but if you were to begin every review like this then it would become clichéd and boring for readers.

Look out for your own 'darlings' and don't be afraid to stamp them out; it will make you a better writer.

4

Writing opinion pieces

Definition

An opinion piece, as its name suggests, is a journalist's opinionated viewpoint. It could be a serious comment piece about politics, or a humorous rant about the confusing, unjust and plain weird state of the world, such as Jeremy Clarkson's writing in the *Sunday Times* or Charlie Brooker in Monday's *Guardian*. Other journalists might use humour to make serious points, such as the *Daily Mail*'s Liz Jones or the *Mirror*'s Tony Parsons.

As this book is intended to give those new to writing journalism a helping hand, this chapter will focus on the serious and humorous types of opinion writing. In my experience of working with groups of aspiring writers, the freedom that writing opinion pieces can allow really helps to develop ideas and individual writing styles.

SERIOUS OPINION

The key difference between opinion writing and almost everything else in a newspaper is that it is driven by a point of view. The serious comment piece is ultimately still opinion, but it can be well substantiated and well argued. The journalist is trying to prove a point and influence debate in their specialist field. They are often fed information from sources as they become known for their viewpoint.

Regular opinion writers with their own weekly columns such as the *Guardian*'s Polly Toynbee or George Monbiot are highly regarded as opinion formers. In the 1990s former Prime Minister Tony Blair recognised the growing importance of these opinion writers when he stated, 'The new technique of comment on the news is as important if not more important than the news itself.'

HUMOROUS OPINION

Humorous opinion writing is also driven by a point of view. Take Clarkson ranting about things that bleep as an example ('Bleep off, you are driving me mad', *Sunday Times*, Sept 2007). It is his characteristic grumpy old man tone that makes such a piece entertaining and readable. The point of view might be flippant, but it is also one of those subjects that will get us all nodding and saying 'Well, he has a point'.

Of course, the opinions of journalists fill our newspapers on a daily basis. If you take nothing else from this book, learning to differentiate between opinion pieces and other forms of journalism will improve your understanding of the media dramatically. As readers, not only do we have to deal with the opinions of journalists, but also of politicians, celebrities, do-gooders, do-badders, rent-a-quotes, people who know a lot and inevitably those who don't.

WHY DO NEWSPAPERS WANT OPINION WRITERS?

The newspaper's view

- Opinion writers like Clarkson and Brooker provide entertainment and an alternative to the heavier 'news pages' with their unrelenting reality.

- Serious opinion writers can get stuck into debates with a greater freedom than news journalists, and can campaign for changes on behalf of their readership. This generates loyalty from readers who see the paper as 'acting on their behalf' or standing up for what they believe in. Think of how the *Sun* got behind the charity Help for Heroes, or the way that many of the newspapers supported greater openness of MP's expenses.

- Opinion columns get readers talking (e.g. 'Did you see what Clarkson wrote this week?'), which is good for boosting circulation.

- Opinion draws the reader into a newspaper and can create reader (i.e. customer) loyalty. Notice how Charlie Brooker in the *Guardian* is consistently the number one 'most read' item on the *Guardian Online* webpage. It is also no accident that his column comes out on a Monday, traditionally the slowest newspaper day as people have often still got the weekend papers to plough through.

- The rise of blogging is changing opinion writing. The internet allows 'citizen journalists' to get their views across about whatever topic they want. Many journalists have made their name this way, including Charlie Brooker whose 'Screenwipe' column began as a blog that was picked up by the *Guardian Guide*.

The reader's view

■ Opinion provides a chance to be outraged, delighted, shocked, gobsmacked, offended, and then to shout it across the office to your workmates.

■ Serious opinion is thought provoking and offers a different angle from what MPs, the government or the corporate world are trying to convince us is true.

■ A good opinion writer articulates what you are thinking, which could be a serious concern but equally could be funny, ridiculous or, if it's in the *Daily Mail* or your local paper, a bit scary.

The writer's view

■ Opinion writing provides a chance to vent your feelings and opinions.

■ It also offers the chance to influence public opinion.

■ Perhaps most importantly, it can provide a regular income without having to leave the desk and do the usual legwork that journalism entails. This is truer for the humorists than the serious opinion writers who need to be well informed and aware of changing issues.

BUT ISN'T JOURNALISM SUPPOSED TO BE OBJECTIVE?

Well actually the 'objective' writing (which we'll deal with in the next chapter on the News) in fact makes up a relatively-small part of newspaper and magazine output – usually just the first couple of pages. Even then, the choice of story is often decided by a set of news values, which will be unique to that organisation. As an aspiring writer, it is important to remember that we seek to achieve objectivity, whilst understanding that there are limitations on that.

CONNECTIONS

In writing serious or humorous opinion journalism it helps if you are well informed and connected so that you hear of goings on amongst movers and shakers. This is the case with George Monbiot who writes about the environment for the *Guardian* as well as the 3am girls in the *Mirror*. The information they deal with varies of course but the principle is the same.

WHAT CAN WE LEARN FROM JEREMY CLARKSON?

The best-known opinion writer at the moment is probably Jeremy Clarkson. He writes for the *Sunday Times*, the largest-selling Sunday newspaper. It is worth knowing that he has long been a journalist and specialised in motoring before becoming a presenter of *Top Gear*.

I suspect that even the mere mention of his name had you either smiling or wincing. And that is the point in a nutshell. We are meant to love him or loathe him – he has built his career around dividing opinion. Grumpy old men say, 'Yeah, that's it! You are soooo right'. Teenage girls just shrug and say, 'God, that sounds just like Dad'. Journalists say, 'I could do that' – and they do, but they don't get paid what Clarkson gets paid. Because Clarkson sells papers, and that is an editor's dream – stick his face on the cover with a bah-humbug strap line and you bag another 10,000 copies on a Sunday morning.

NICE WORK IF YOU CAN GET IT

A major factor influencing journalists' aspirations for writing opinion pieces is that this type of writing provides regular work and therefore a regular income. It is also often perceived as easier work. What could be better than writing without the leg work? No calling up disinterested parties and trying to extract a witty quote, no reading through endless crap press releases in the vain search for a good story. Just think of a funny theme – say, smelly socks – and off you go.

Opinion writing exercises

Humorous

Okay, time to try writing an opinion piece for yourself. Choosing a subject should come naturally but, in case it doesn't, think modern irritations: Facebook stalkers, pavement cyclists, pushy parents, the BNP. Or your subject could be an observation: Why do Dads drive buggies one-handed? Do local council employees ever do any work? Does anyone actually watch *Big Brother* live? Why do people wear leg warmers in summer? Let rip your deepest and darkest feelings about any subject – neighbours, bosses, reality television.

Although I am encouraging you to let rip, remember that the piece has to maintain interest and not lose your reader – a golden rule of all journalism is not to be boring. So keep it amusing and pick a topic that has, if not universal appeal, then at least appeal for the audience that you are writing for.

Aim for 300–400 words for your first attempt, and 700–800 words for subsequent pieces.

If you are in doubt about how to start then try parodying the style of Jeremy Clarkson or Charlie Brooker, or one of the many other 'grumpy old men/women' writers who moan about the modern world in a funny and baffled, what the hell is going on, kind of way.

Serious

Taking on an issue that is of particular concern to you is always gratifying and your natural interest can lead to a greater knowledge of and appreciation for all the dimensions of a debate. Remember that your piece should focus on an angle and a point of view and include evidence that backs up your point of view.

If you are struggling to think of an idea, look through your local newspaper and identify a key issue in your area. Perhaps it is the behaviour of your local council or a local company which is laying off staff. Try and think of an argument that hasn't been articulated by your paper, or try taking the opposing view of an argument that it has published.

Further reading
Humorous:

- Charlie Brooker in the *Guardian*.

- Jeremy Clarkson in the *Sunday Times*.

- Tony Parsons in the *Mirror*.

- Liz Jones in the *Daily Mail*.

Serious:

- Andreas Whittam Smith who writes about finance in the *Independent*.

- David Wighton, the business editor for *The Times*.

- George Monbiot who writes about the environment for the *Guardian*.

5

And now for the news

Definition

News is fact-driven, timely reporting on real life events. It can be sub-divided into many types: global news, European news, national news, local news. Into niche types of news: business news, financial news, property news. And even more niche than that: cycling news, printers' news, books news and so on.

Nowadays we are surrounded by news 'as it happens' 24/7. Its ubiquitous nature means that almost everyone is familiar with the structure of news writing, either consciously or unconsciously. One of the great clichés about news writing is that 'facts are sacred'. This is obvious, but as the media has become increasingly opinionated, celebrity and lifestyle-driven, it is important to remember the distinction between those kinds of journalism and news writing.

News writing starts with the most relevant information and works its way down to the least relevant. This is known as 'the inverted pyramid', which we will look at in more detail below. First, let's begin with the question, What is news?

WHAT IS NEWS?

Opposite of olds! News has to be, by its very nature, new information, time relevant and also relevant to the particular audience that is picking up the paper or 'tuning in'.

News is also fact based. Further into a newspaper, the implications of news events might be discussed but on the front page, to quote another brilliant journalistic cliché, 'facts are king'.

WHERE IS NEWS FOUND?

My first job in journalism was writing the news for a local radio station in Sheffield. Religiously, every morning would start with phone calls to pre-recorded answer machines with up-to-date incident information from the police, local council, fire station and hospitals. No wonder then that much of the local news is so cheery.

Press offices, RSS feeds, newsletters and press agencies are churning out potential stories all the time. If you are looking for stories, I recommend signing up for as much as possible. You will always have to wade through rubbish to find that gem, but that is just part of the process.

Depending upon your particular niches and interests you may wish to look into some of the following:

■ Local council feeds – nationals won't always be aware of what is happening in your area, but with your finger on the pulse you will be able to alert them.

- Facebook has so many groups and fan pages for many different types of organisations and groups, from the mainstream to the miniscule. These will feed automatically into your 'Newsfeed' page and keep you updated with what is going on.

- University and hospital press offices are usually very active and will issue press releases for upcoming events and academic or medical research.

All over the place and over time news journalists build up a list of contacts – people who they know they can call on to have a chat and see if anything has 'cropped up'. This doesn't need to result in hard-hitting news every time – a feature or a profile from such a source would be welcome to the freelancer reliant on getting paid by the word.

What makes news?

What makes news depends largely upon the criteria of the publication. What is news for the *Sun* is a world away from news for your local newspaper. But, broadly speaking, the nationals look largely to politics and economics, whereas regional and local papers always lead with crime, council politics and court cases.

You can see from these types of criteria why people talk of 'negative news values'. This is basically the idea that bad news is the only news, but it is in fact the way that news is gathered that influences the stories that are run.

STRUCTURE OF NEWS

A classic structure for how to write news is 'the inverted pyramid'. This diagram is designed to emphasise that a news piece begins with the most vital information and works its way down to the least important.

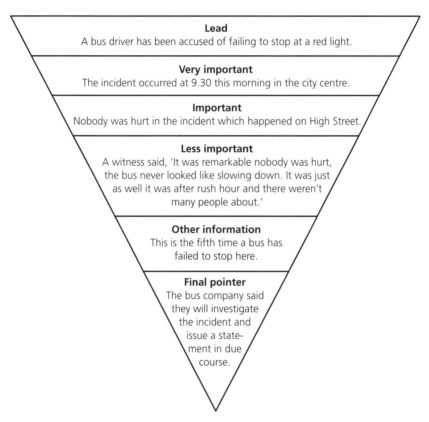

Lead
A bus driver has been accused of failing to stop at a red light.

Very important
The incident occurred at 9.30 this morning in the city centre.

Important
Nobody was hurt in the incident which happened on High Street.

Less important
A witness said, 'It was remarkable nobody was hurt, the bus never looked like slowing down. It was just as well it was after rush hour and there weren't many people about.'

Other information
This is the fifth time a bus has failed to stop here.

Final pointer
The bus company said they will investigate the incident and issue a statement in due course.

READERSHIP

It is important to remember that the most relevant information will depend upon the audience for the news. For example, for a local audience this would be, 'Local man bludgeoned to death', whereas the same story in a national might report, 'Fifth murder in a week as UK murder rate continues to rise'. Both stories would then continue with the other news essentials, i.e. Who was the victim? When did the incident occur? Is there a suspected motive or are the police looking for anyone in particular for questioning?

The 'final pointer' is the little hook to entice you to 'stay tuned'. The classic example is, 'The case continues next week' but it could also be 'Detectives are investigating the scene and more details will be released in the morning'.

PRESSURES ON NEWS WRITING

Deadlines are of course the persistent pressure and, depending on the publication, they could be daily, three times a day, weekly, monthly or quarterly.

The need for visual images is also a common pressure, especially for TV news for which a reporter might, for example, stand outside a hospital reporting on something that took place inside several hours ago. Visual images bring life into newspapers and capture people's attention. Hence the classic technique of bringing in a model to open a supermarket – otherwise why would anyone want to read about a supermarket being opened?

HOW DO WE REMAIN OBJECTIVE?

There is a common belief that all news is objective. Yet it could be argued that if a journalist is faced with a choice of 20 stories a day, the very fact that he or she is choosing to write one story over another is a subjective decision. Journalists decide what they think an audience is interested in and obviously there is never time to find out if this is really the case.

In addition, deadlines are a reality of the journalist's working life and everything has to be done by the 'end of play' – whether that is later in the day, or at the end of the week or month. Realistically, if you tackle a story with the intention of providing as many voices as is practical then you have done your job. You can't interview every single witness to an incident if there are 30, but you can speak to four and report the one that you feel reflects the general view.

News writing exercise

What is going on in your local area? News isn't passionate and heartfelt – it is a list of facts of what happened, when and who was involved. Adopt an old fashioned hard-boiled New York editor's voice and tell yourself to 'Stick to the facts'.

Aim for 150–250 words and imagine that this piece is for your local paper. Keep it relevant to the people of your town and the kinds of things that they are likely to want to know about.

If you are struggling to find a story, read back over the 'Where is news found?' section above and follow your curiosity. Lots of press releases can be found online under the 'News' or 'Press' sections of websites of, for example, local councils or universities. Find something that you think is interesting and look for quotes that can be used to make your piece as realistic as possible. You can also try looking for ideas in your local paper and BBC website.

Interview: **Richard Cookson**

Investigative journalist Richard Cookson talks about some tricks of his trade and making the transition to broadcast journalism.

Richard Cookson is a freelance investigative journalist with over ten years' experience. He specialises in foreign affairs, social affairs and the environment, and has worked for a wide range of national newspapers and broadcasters. His written work has appeared in the *Daily Mail*, the *Guardian*, the *Independent*, *Independent on Sunday*, the *Observer*, *Private Eye* and a range of magazines. He has also worked on Channel 4's programmes *Dispatches* and *Unreported World*, and the BBC's *Inside Out*.

What is investigative journalism?

Nick Davies, the *Guardian*'s investigative journalist tells this story: Two people are in a room and a journalist asks, 'What is the weather like?' One person replies that it is sunny, the other that it is raining.

Conventional journalism would say, 'Controversy reigns as two experts clash in discussion about the weather', whereas in investigative reporting, the journalist just goes and looks out of the window and finds out it is sunny. Then they will question why one person has said it is raining and will discover that they are the owner of an umbrella manufacturing company or whatever.

So in essence, investigative journalists are trying to get to 'a truth' – whatever that may be. The key thing is that investigative journalism needs to be driven by the public interest.

Which areas do you specialise in?

Largely social affairs, but also the environment and more recently foreign affairs.

Can you explain why investigative journalism is so important?
Well, it works for the public interest. But I'd also add that it is
needed now more than ever before, as there is a hugely-resourced
PR machine out there trying to persuade us of all sorts of things.

Investigative reporting has uncovered some incredible things –
classic cases include the thalidomide scandal broken by the *Sunday
Times* in the 1970s. More recently we have had MPs' expenses
exposed which led to a Lords' enquiry and MPs having to pay
back money they weren't entitled to.

The media itself is another example. There was one case of
journalists exposing a reality show that was 'stunted'. That is a
good example of where a lot of resources had been deployed but
the journalists got to the truth.

**What would be a good place to start for someone interested in
investigative reporting?**
It is difficult as revenues are being squeezed and circulations are
dropping. Investigative journalism takes time and a lot of money,
so it is an easy target for the bean counters.

Investigative journalists generally come up through news writing
so that is a great starting point. To my mind, all journalism
should ask difficult questions. So you need to learn the basics of
your trade.

**How does investigative journalism differ from other forms of
journalism?**
You have to have a solid understanding of the basics of news
journalism: what makes a story, how to produce a story. All the
media law stuff is incredibly important, as you are challenging
powerful people and questioning them about things that they will
sue you over.

You need to be patient and methodical. A lot of it is about trawling
through 100-page documents and maintaining your focus so you
don't have to re-read things.

At some point you are going to have to talk to people and get information from them that they may not want to immediately share. So you have to work out strategies for getting information out of people.

Such as?
The thing I find most useful is imagining being in their shoes and what I would do in their situation. Why would I tell a journalist some information? Many people have very noble motivations and you have to appeal to those. An investigative journalist may take weeks in getting someone to open up to them.

Do editors recognise the extra time you have taken and pay you accordingly?
Yes, but not always. The good editors recognise that you have spent longer and will pay more. But I find the best way to earn reasonable money is to publish multiple articles and then also to publish subsequent follow-ups – and across as many types of media as possible.

I try and do a range of different work, some of which might not be investigative. I really try and ensure that I have several investigative pieces on the go at the same time. One of the most important principles is also being able to let go of something if you find it isn't worth pursuing.

How have you made the transition from print to broadcasting?
I had been doing a very lengthy piece of work on an ex-police informer who died in a way that really troubled his parents. They went through all the paperwork and things just didn't stack up, so they called me. It turned out the parents had been treated very badly and the inquest was criticised very heavily.

So I pitched this story to a Channel 4 programme. They didn't take that particular story, but it did lead to some work on *Dispatches*. I started by researching stories and then writing them up into pitch documents, and I have gone on to learn how to use a camera.

Do a lot of people in broadcasting come from a journalism background?
Very few actually, many are through-and-through TV people. They have taken the traditional route of runners to assistant producers and worked up from there. I was surprised at how few journalists there are but that works well for me, although I have had to work hard to get up to speed on the broadcasting side.

Who are the journalists that you admire?
Certainly Nick Davies from the *Guardian*. He has an incredible ability to get to the heart of stories, as his work on phone tapping at News International proves.

I also have a lot of respect for Rob Evans who also works at the *Guardian* and who I am lucky to have worked with. Again, he regularly produces hard-hitting work. When I was growing up, Peter Cook of *The Cook Report* was on TV and I used to be glued to that.

Do you have any other advice for aspiring journalists?
I think that although there isn't much money around, we as journalists need to work hard to keep all this alive. And there is nothing to stop people doing longer, in-depth pieces of work alongside their day jobs.

If I worked out my hourly rate sometimes it would be eye-watering, but journalists are there to help people understand what is happening in the world and if we are not doing that then we are failing ourselves.

The other thing to say is that with the arrival of new electronic resources, the core is never going to change but there is an incredible amount of information out there. And I really hope that these tools re-invigorate investigative journalism in what is a time of incredible transition.

Journalism is so valuable to society that we can't afford to let it die out, and I am sure we won't.

6

Feature writing

Definition

A feature explores a subject or issue in more depth and is therefore a longer piece of writing. It is often driven by an interview, debate or unfolding story.

Features are the lifeblood of magazines, making up a large percentage of their content. Writing features is the aim of many freelance journalists; a quick look at a few freelance journalists' directories online reveals that the majority include feature writing as one of their specialisms. As most publications pay rates that are based on the number of words or the hundreds of words, it follows that journalists make a better living as a feature journalist.

Like many journalists, I worked up to features after spending some time doing smaller pieces. I wrote several before deciding to invest in myself and I enrolled on a two-day course on feature writing at the NUJ (National Union of Journalists). Despite being several years ago now, the course has stayed with me and provided a blueprint for much of my feature writing.

As a result, most of this chapter is due to Brendan Foley from the NUJ who has kindly allowed me to draw on his work. He is interviewed below and still runs the two-day feature writing course at the NUJ in London, which I can't recommend highly enough.

WHAT IS A FEATURE?

The first thing to consider with a feature article is what are the defining characteristics of this kind of journalism and what makes it different from the other types of journalism that we have already looked at? I think it is fair to say that features provide a wider discussion, which could be person-based (a celebrity for example), news-based (the wider implications of a new development), or subject- or issue-based (Can we ever learn to live without fossil fuels? Are celebrities all freaks?).

The major difference is the involvement of *people* in the development and writing of a feature: politicians, business people, musicians, film stars, minor celebrities, protestors, local people. Getting out there and bringing others into the equation always brings its own challenges, but we will deal with some of these later.

TWO SIDES TO A STORY?

In news writing, we discussed how it was important to provide more than one viewpoint in an attempt to be as objective as possible. Brendan Foley suggests that there are often *three* sides to a story. Think of it in terms of a debate: one speaker supports a motion while another argues against it, but Foley believes that a third 'alternative' viewpoint completes a story.

So if you were writing a feature discussing the value of freelance journalism training books, you might have a grizzly old hack suggesting that the only way to learn is to start at the bottom at a local newspaper. Your second opinion might be from someone like me saying, 'This book will teach you everything you ever need to know, and every aspiring journalist should own at least two copies.' So far, so predictable. But your third source might be an editor who says, 'I used to waste weeks telling new starters about the basics of journalism. Now I tell them to read Leverton's book before they start work and I save our company thousands in wasted man hours.'

RESEARCHING AND DOUBLE-CHECKING

Research is basically finding as much out about a subject as you can. There is always a danger that you will bog yourself down with too much information, but see the interview techniques later in this chapter for one way of dealing with this.

An inevitable human trait is being selective with information – this is as true for you as it is for your subject. You have to decide what is the most important information and present it as clearly and concisely as possible. You also need to know that this information is correct and that you aren't ignorantly sailing into shark-infested waters where you are going to find yourself mauled, sued and left for dead in the water.

The solution is to double-check information. If you have researched something from the internet, cross-reference it with a book or an expert in the field. If you speak to an expert in the field, check it with someone else to make sure you aren't being spun a line.

A scientist may tell you of a new breakthrough that will change the way we treat patients. Some further investigation may reveal that this scientist's research is being paid for by a big multinational pharmaceutical company which is aiming to corner the market for the treatment. I am not suggesting that you need to run some kind of exposé when faced with this information. You can simply write, for example, 'Leverton Drugs International funded research has shown that everyone in the world needs to buy this new cure-all; however GP Bob Smith suggests, 'It is still too early to tell if these drugs will make any impact.' This should be sufficient for an intelligent reader to draw their own conclusions as to how impartial the new findings are.

Along with double-checking, also make sure that you state facts (which are referenced or quoted and that you can provide evidence for later if needs be). If you do this, then you should be fine.

The easiest way to research is always by speaking to people (see Interview Techniques below). If you are frantically trying to learn about crop rotation for an article and have never even been to the countryside, it would be better to find some kindly farmer who doesn't mind talking to you in layperson's terms than trying to interpret some dry information from Wikipedia.

If you are writing for a general audience, they will appreciate being told about something in language that they can understand. Even an educated audience will find a clearly-written article easier to read and will stick with you until you quote a new piece of information they didn't know.

Publication research

It is essential that you know your publication and readership (see Chapter 2, 'Who is the audience?'). You might remember the anecdote in Chapter 1 about the man who would phone *The Big Issue*, trying to get his fiction published in a current affairs magazine. This highlights the basis of publication research and my advice can be summed up as simply as 'read your target publication'.

If you read the publication and look at what types of articles they publish then you should be halfway there. But also look at what they don't publish – if there are no reviews of films, it is pointless telling them that you hope to be the next Mark Kermode.

Researching a story

As well as researching the publication you are writing for, it is necessary to research the topic, person or organisation you are writing about.

Getting the balance right is the key here. Too much research and you can get yourself bogged down in the issue and find yourself sick of it before you even start writing. Not enough research and whoever you speak to will soon tell. This might not be a huge problem. People generally understand that journalists can't be experts in every sphere of human activity. It is only a problem if you miss something important that they say because you didn't really understand it at the time.

I once interviewed someone from a well-known building society that went bust at the start of the credit crunch. They started off talking to me as if they were in a meeting with a group of chief executives. I turned it around by saying, 'I know what you are telling me, but bearing in mind that a lot of our readers are laypeople in financial issues, would you mind explaining that again in a way that is understandable to the man in the street?' The interviewee graciously re-worded his point so that the readers (and I) were able to comprehend it.

PLAN BEFORE YOU WRITE

In his course, Brendan Foley stresses the importance of planning a feature before starting any writing. As such, he encourages students to sketch out a plan that could look something like this. Remember his advice of presenting three sides to a story.

Introduction – Leverton Drugs International: rip off or life-savers? (Find a strong opening quote.) (125 words)

A – Director of Leverton (250 words)

B – Head of campaign group: 'Death to Leverton Drugs International' (250 words)

C – Woman whose life was saved after drug treatment: 'All my hair fell out and I turned green, but I am still alive.' (250 words)

Conclusion – Saved lives, but at what cost? (125 words)
(End quote 'I am suing Leverton Drugs,' says the green woman.)

Total word count: 1000 words

Now that you have an idea of what you want from your article, you can plan and position your questions accordingly. Importantly, the word count dictates how much time you can spend talking to each source. This isn't rigid and can be moved around to suit the best quotes. We will look at this later in the chapter, along with other things to be aware of when conducting an interview.

THE NUTS AND BOLTS OF FEATURE WRITING

Introduction

The purpose of an introduction is to introduce a story, but not necessarily immediately. Notice how in some articles the journalist brings you into a bit of 'back story' first and then possibly returns to it later in the piece. This technique creates a little more drama and colour than just simply stating the obvious. Sometimes it is appropriate, and you have only the word count, only to state the obvious but keep a look out for this technique as it is very effective.

Framing a story with a 'human interest' angle is another common technique. Before leading the reader through the main areas of debate around parking tickets, for example, you may wish to introduce Bob the traffic warden:

> 'I have been shouted at, punched, kicked and spat at,' explains traffic warden Bob Billet. 'I have no faith left in civilised society – we should ban the motor car,' he says with a shake of his head.

Using a powerful quote grabs your reader's attention and encourages them to read on.

Key paragraph

This section states what the article is going to do and where it will go. For example:

> 'Leverton Drugs International has been in the news for its groundbreaking yet controversial treatments. We speak to the company, medical experts and patients to discover what lies behind the Leverton empire.'

Quotes

The essence of journalism is people – people want to know about other people: what they think, what they feel, what they like, etc. This is what we want to find out about from features and it is the journalist's job not to stand in front of their subject but to allow the subject to take centre stage. The journalist is stage-managing the whole thing or directing it, but the reader wants to hear the voices and make their own mind up.

A quote can transform a piece and lift it from being informative yet dull to being a thrilling read.

> 'All that I ever wanted was for people to take what I say seriously,' said the comedian with a tear in his eye.

This quote shows what a bit of emotion can do. It can grab our interest and compel us to read on in a way that a dry bit of text can't. Remember to maintain interest; a journalist should never allow a reader to become bored. Adding the right quotes in the right place will help you keep hold of your reader to the final word in the piece.

How to quote

Students often ask if they can change the words of someone they have interviewed. Quotes can be changed only so that they make sense when read. People do not speak in a way that makes sense on the printed page. We slip between tenses, say 'um', 'er' and drift off at the end of a sentence, and tend to say 'You know what I mean?' So quotes can be changed to make the interviewee sound better in this sense, and people will actually expect you to make them sound better. But you cannot change the essence of what someone meant in a sentence.

This may seem like a fine line to tread but the golden rule is to stay true to the meaning and make it read well.

If you have interviewed someone properly then you will inevitably have too much material to include in your article. So you have to choose which quotes you are going to put in and which you are going to leave out. This is an editing process and often you will find that certain quotes simply must go in and then the rest need to fit in around the plan that you have already established.

Quotes are often used at the beginning of an article to provide a punchy dramatic introduction, or they can be used for similar effects at the close of a piece. They could also leave the reader with a wistful thought, a question or an emotion. This leads to understanding one of the most important functions of quotes: providing emotion.

Adding emotion

Where quotes can really lift a piece is in the delivery of some emotion. The nitty gritty of explaining what is going on is the job of the journalist, as is setting the scene and finding some statistics to support what is being stated. But it is still a crime to be boring, and listening to one voice for long periods of time inevitably becomes dull and monotonous.

> 'My mother always told me I had too much to say for myself, and that I liked the sound of my own voice,' said the journalist when asked about his new book.

Signposts

Signposting in writing is like those annoying re-cap bits in TV programmes that come on after a commercial break, cheerfully reminding you what happened in the first ten minutes of the show (just in case your short-term memory was failing and you couldn't remember that Phil and Kirsty have been to a house and are about to go to another house). Seriously though, signposting is very necessary in large chunks of text so that your reader is given a moment or two to digest the information and is encouraged to read on. So a signpost may sound something like this:

> 'Now we have looked at the basic requirements of feature writing, we are in a position to move on to some of the more advanced techniques.'

Thus, the 'signpost' indicates where you have been, and where you are heading to from this point.

Maintaining interest is one of the most difficult things to achieve in feature writing. Think about how you consume an article yourself – we are all guilty of flicking through, skim reading and picking the interesting things out, maybe just reading the 'pull quotes' (see Appendix 1, Jargon Buster). With this in mind, it is your job to stop the reader from flicking through and to make them want to read your piece, so you must keep driving the story forward before they can get bored.

Outro

You have to leave the reader satisfied that you have covered everything you said you were going to. Have you answered all of the questions you raised in your introduction? Often a reader will cheat and go straight to the final paragraph to see how the article ends; if their curiosity is significantly aroused they may go back and read the rest of your piece. So the conclusion needs to sum up your discussion. But you may also decide that a question is more effective. Or some kind of nod to the future: 'Will these changes spell the end of the traditional journalism industry? Or can it re-invent itself in the coming decades to compete with the online revolution?'

You have been on a little journey with your reader but now it is time to say goodbye. Remember how we laughed at the funny quote, sighed at the inevitable consequences and were annoyed at the arrogance of those quotes. As she was ushered out of the door by suited minders she turned to me and said, 'Finish my article with a stunning quote, one that makes the hairs on the back of your neck stand up.'

Feature writing exercise

Remember that a feature is the 'next step up' for writers. If a full feature still seems very daunting, go back and write more reviews until you feel ready to tackle something larger.

If you have a burning idea for something that you want to write about, then crack on with it. Remember Brendan Foley's advice of writing a plan before you put pen to paper or finger to key.

Also remember that a feature is a rounded or balanced story: you will need to speak to people, show contrasting viewpoints and take your reader on a little journey.

If you are seeking some inspiration for your first feature, think through some of the following:

- Do I know anyone with an unusual job?

- Do I know someone who is a bit of a local celebrity?

■ Is there someone who has had an unusual experience? For example, someone who has had a sex change, been abducted by aliens, has stood for parliament, invented a piece of software or served in a war?

■ Is there an issue that I would like people to have a greater understanding of? And would like to get a greater understanding of myself?

Features average 800–1,200 words in most magazines and newspapers. Aim for the shorter length to begin with. Remember less is sometimes more and although you might have lots of material it doesn't mean you have to use it all. If you were baking a cake, throwing in more and more ingredients wouldn't make it taste any better.

Study a feature writer

There are hundreds of feature writers out there. Whatever your area of interest, try and find a writer who regularly contributes to a publication and see if you can work out if they are using some kind of formula. Google them, find out what you can about their career, how they started and what else they have written.

Analyse their work and see if you can find techniques they use regularly. Imagine what pitch they made to the editor and from where they sourced their quotes. This will help you get under the skin of a writer and imagine what they are doing to create their work.

INTERVIEW TECHNIQUES

Interviews are a conversation with a purpose. You need to gain certain information for your article and the interviewee will often have certain information that they want to give to you. Balancing these demands is part of the skill of the interviewing process and until you start to speak to someone, you have no idea what kind of interview they are going to give.

Preparation for an interview

Preparation is paramount: know something about your subject. You don't need to be well versed in every last detail of someone's career but it is polite to be aware of the basics. The more ignorant you are, the less likely it is that they will want to share that special nugget of information which could make your piece stand out.

Prepare some questions but remember you don't have to stick to them rigidly. However in the worst-case scenario, in which you become completely tongue-tied by the beauty or arrogance of your subject, it is good to be able to just read out the questions and get the job done if you have to. If this happens, hopefully you will be able to read out the questions but also remain alert enough to pick up on any interesting elements that your subject refers to in the course of the interview.

The questions themselves should be based on the classic 'who, what, where, when, why and how'. But only you will know what is the most relevant in each specific case. If you are speaking to someone who is jumping out of an aeroplane, we will need to know who, where and when. The 'how?' might be answered with 'dressed as a chicken', but the 'why' can reveal a personal story which takes the article to another level: 'A chicken saved my life when I tried to cross a particularly busy road and for that reason I will never eat another chicken, and I am raising money for the charity Chickens 4 Life.' Tomorrow the headline reads, 'The *Post* reveals why the chicken crossed the road' by I. M. Brilliant.

Following up on responses

Another thing to consider when asking a series of questions is how people might respond. I often warm the subject up with a couple of boring questions:

- How do you spell your name?

- What is your job title?

- How would you like to be referred to?

If you were dealing with someone famous or with a busy chief executive you might want to get these kinds of details from a press officer or a PA. But if you are speaking with someone 'normal', then getting the person talking and comfortable with talking to you is going to make your life easier.

One of the worst-case scenarios is interviewing someone who is monosyllabic, giving you 'yes' and 'no' answers. Asking open questions can help to encourage people to speak at more length, so instead of:

Interviewer: 'Do you think you are great?'

Interviewee: 'Oh yes.'

ask:

Interviewer: 'What is it that makes you so great?'

Interviewee: 'Well I was born to make music. The good lord gave me that gift and my parents helped me when I was a child to make the world a better place by shaking my booty.'

Brendan Foley's advice is to ask just six to eight questions and he divides these into:

- need to know;

- like to know;

- danger zone.

Need to know is the stuff you have to have: the person's name, what they are doing, when they are doing it.

Like to know is the whys and wherefores: digging a bit deeper, finding out about their motivations and inspirations, their fears and desires.

Danger zone is the area where you might just be pushing your luck a little bit, and if you aren't careful your interviewee might respond by hanging up or walking out on you. You may well be thinking, 'Well if that is the risk, why the hell would you do that?' That is a good question and you would be right to ask it, but very often people don't like to open up immediately to a journalist. Rightly so, they don't know where you've been.

However, remember the points covered above about the value of good strong quotes to an article. If you give people a nudge, they often reply with that bit of passion or oomph that you are looking for. They stop trying to be polite and instead get straight to the point: 'The only time I have ever worn women's clothing was for Children in Need,' said the vicar.

Keeping control of the interview

It happens frequently that an interviewee with a forceful personality can go on and on, while you struggle to get a word in edgeways. If you literally can't get a word in, try using body language: hold your hand up or just interrupt with 'Yes, that is a good point *but* unfortunately I have only limited space so can we move on to talk about the next stage of your life?'

I remember very clearly letting one of my early interviewees talk and talk. It was so much fun, talking to them didn't seem like work – it was just a chat, outside on a nice sunny day. But then came the transcription.

TRANSCRIPTION

Transcription is the process of writing up a recorded interview into a literal translation ready for using to write your piece. Nowadays I am confident enough just to listen through and pick out the quotes that I want for an article, but this hasn't always been the case. I remember being afraid I would miss something and so spent many hours transcribing interviews in full – the very pleasant two-hour conversation I had with an interviewee out in the sun, for example, resulted in a painful afternoon of transcription.

My typing speed has also improved and I can now keep up with most talking speeds, but when I began I used to have to factor in a pretty poor ratio of twice the length of the interview for transcription. This illustrates why you need to retain control of your interviews. As a freelancer, your time is money, so save your precious time as much as you can by preparing for interviews and staying in control of them.

SHOULD I LEARN SHORTHAND?

I have been frequently asked whether it's worth learning shorthand. The main purpose of this skill is again to save time. I didn't learn shorthand because I find recording an interview to be less intrusive and because I prefer to focus on just one thing at a time. Writing notes, listening and asking questions all at the same time would probably make my head explode. So I keep things simple by having a list of pre-prepared questions and a record function on my mobile phone that catches everything for me.

Interview: **Brendan Foley**

Feature writer Brendan Foley shares some of his experiences and discusses the current state of journalism.

Brendan Foley has been a journalist since the age of 15. He has worked as a press officer, an editor, and nowadays devotes his time to script writing. He has had several scripts produced by Hollywood including the *The Riddle*, which stars Vinnie Jones. He also runs fantastic two-day feature writing courses at the National Union of Journalists (NUJ).

www.brendan.foley.btinternet.co.uk

How did you start?
I started as what I thought was a freelance but I was more of a mascot at the *Belfast Telegraph*. I thought I was adding something but I was probably just being amused by the journalists. This was in the late 70s and 80s – I would have been a copy boy in the old days.

From that I went to University in York and when I came out it was one of the many journalistic downturns, so I freelanced out of necessity. I then went to the corporate side of the fence, working in PR and then as an editor.

How important is having a specialism?
You have to have a specialism as a freelance. People have to go to you for a specific reason. If it is general copy, they will have someone in house who can deal with that. So mine has been business, environment and some conflict stuff. I did have a very specific specialism at one stage: the oil industry in danger zones. So I was writing about companies all over the world and travelling a lot. These things are driven by global economic factors.

In economic terms, no paper is going to send a freelance to Angola. But a business would and so I would use that situation to write stories for business magazines and national newspapers that are interested in eyewitness accounts. If you are a freelance, you have to look for ways to re-jig ideas into different publications.

So you have seen downturns like our present one before?
I have seen this kind of downturn before and it happens in journalism. I think the industry is like a big dog with fleas – after a while it gets up and has a shake. As freelances, we fall into the flea category, but the good thing is that the world is full of dogs! As a freelance, you have to realise that it isn't about you personally, it is about how you adapt to the market conditions.

You also need to write about what you know – that old truism – but adapt it to what people want to read.

What kind of people take your course?
Feature writing is rarely taught, and more and more journalists are coming into the industry through what they used to call the 'non-traditional route', to the extent to which you are now unusual if you have taken the traditional NCTJ (National Council for the Training of Journalists) formal training route.

Is this a good or a bad thing?

The lack of formal training is no good thing in my opinion, but it is good that the NUJ is one of the main providers of quality short courses. If you use the BBC as an analogy, it used to be that everyone would learn there and only some would move on. It seems now that the burden of training is falling onto the individual. That is just the reality.

Is there one thing that always gets a good reaction on your course?

The stuff I do on feature structure, without a doubt. Students might have been writing for some time and are paranoid of being outed. The structure isn't a straitjacket, it is just a guide. The other thing to understand is that everything has a beginning, middle and end. And I had a group recently that got excited when I said you have to know what you are writing, for who and when.

Freelances also need to recharge their batteries every now and then, so it is about re-injecting some enthusiasm back into their writing. This enthusiasm often leads to more work.

It is especially important for freelances to realise that they need to work out how much they are getting paid.

Have you noticed anything else about the industry from your students?

Many freelances don't make a good living and have very supportive partners. The work itself can pay less than working at McDonalds, and the industry is sustained by these people working part-time. The world has to recognise that there are people who have fought their way into being freelance journalists. I admire people who attain the skills come hell or high water.

Is it true that there is more pressure from PR these days?

I think it is greater than people think: in the UK there are approximately 50,000 mainstream journalists and 60,000 people working in PR. Communication is communication and you can work in PR and have integrity, and you can work in journalism and not have integrity. There are always pressures to play whatever tune someone wants you to play – it is a tightrope.

Is working freelance becoming more of a norm these days?
I think we are ahead of the curve in seeing the effects of
casualisation. You might have to be tactical – it isn't full-time
freelance or bust.

**Despite these concerns do you have any other advice for aspiring
journalists?**
You need to like people and be amused by their complexities and
idiosyncrasies. There is nothing better than being challenged by
new ideas and new people. Being a journalist is like a permanent
Blue Peter special assignment but the price of the ticket is very high.

7

Travel writing

Definition

Travel sections of newspapers and magazines include many styles of writing and cover almost every style of journalism described in this book, ranging from a news section providing up-to-date news from the travel industry to an opinion piece that describes funny and unfortunate events that can befall the traveller. There may be reviews of travel-related products, services or destinations.

Most people, when they think of travel writing, tend to forget about the wide variety of travel writing possible and remember only the longer feature-length articles. Often it is a long journey in a far-away land that is described and there is a good reason why newspapers publish such articles – namely, armchair travel.

It is easy to think of 'travel writing' only in terms of books by Bill Bryson and the like. But there are many classic travel writers such as Paul Theroux, Jan Morris and Eric Newby, who an aspiring travel writer should be aware of, even though there is a distinction between journalism and wider travel writing. In a broad sense, both of these forms of writing are aiming to achieve a sense of armchair travel. Most travel writing in newspapers, for example, appears in the weekend supplements when we are ready to take our minds off work and are seeking a bit of escapism. Having said that though, looking through the weekend travel supplements also throws up a lot of content that is more factual.

Interestingly the interview towards the end of this chapter with Simon Calder, Editor of *The Independent Traveller* magazine, reveals that the majority of pitches he receives are for full features. Looking for openings in smaller sections is a great alternative way in – you can build up a relationship with the editor over time, prove that you can come up with good copy, hit your deadlines and show that you are worth a punt on a larger feature at a later date. The other benefit of writing a small section in a large magazine is that it gives you the opportunity to say, for example, 'I write for *The Independent Traveller*' and to use this to find work with other similar titles. You aren't stretching the truth by making this kind of statement.

HOW TO WRITE LIKE A TRAVEL JOURNALIST

The travel writer relies on the classic who, why, how, what, when of traditional journalism, but also borrows from the novelist in looking for ways in which to engage the senses. 'The smell of fresh flowers, mixed with the clean fresh breeze meandering in off the snow-capped mountain' would immediately transport you away from a wet Sunday morning in Croydon.

Evoking a sense of place relies on engaging as many of the senses as possible. Many travel writers can connect with the visual element, as this comes easily to us from our camera training. But what can make the difference is looking beyond the surface impressions of a place. Adding a quote from a local, or even a snippet of an overheard conversation can contribute a great deal, as does bringing in the sense of smell such as I did above in a way that is slightly less clichéd than a simple visual image of 'the snow-capped mountain'.

Same rules apply

Travel writing spans every style of journalism and can be news- or interview-led, or written as a feature or in the common 'guide' style. So you can combine what you have learnt in other chapters with a travel element.

Style and approach will be dictated by the readership. *Condé Nast Travel* might not be the best magazine to approach with a feature about where to find free parties in South East Asia. But this could work as a travel feature in a youth-led magazine such as *Wallpaper* in which the editorial focuses are on travel, design, entertainment, fashion and media. *Wallpaper* also have a lot of online content and produce city guidebooks for over 60 cities.

HOW TO MAKE THE MOST OF
TRAVELLING AS A WRITER

Like music writers, travel writers suffer from the curse of there being more people wanting to do the job than there are real opportunities. This doesn't make it impossible to achieve, it just makes it harder – but travellers are probably the kind of people who enjoy a challenge anyway.

There is a myth that travel writers are people who get paid to travel, which probably isn't strictly true. I would suggest that for the majority, travel comes first and making some money from some travel writing as you go would be an additional bonus. That isn't to say I haven't heard of people who have bagged a great deal of free stuff from setting up blogs that document their trips. However, tales like these tend to be the exception rather than the norm.

Travel editors are always going to be looking for stories from people who are actually in a location or who have just returned. Being there offers an advantage insomuch as your editor could email you asking you to go and check a new hotel, for example, which might add an exciting element to your trip and contribute to your travel funds.

This is worth thinking about in greater depth. When I went travelling myself, I consciously didn't think of my career back home, but if you were wanting to travel and write at the same time it might be worth doing some research about places to write about before you actually travel to them. Researching and planning a trip is also a great way to pass those frustrating last few months before you set sail. You will probably have greater access to the internet and the time for thinking about various angles and seeing what has already been written about by your chosen publications.

Make a speculative approach

You could make a speculative approach by sending out some preliminary emails to see if you capture an editor's interest. Most travel editors I have encountered tend to be incredibly busy and have emails coming at them from every direction, but it is always worth a go.

Before you do this think through your approach to the story, for example:

'I am about to take a trip to South America. I will be taking in the usual stops but also plan to do some surfing. I wondered if you might be interested in a piece that looks at the surfing hot spots. I will also be able to supply photos.'

PRESS TRIPS

Another myth surrounding travel writing is that of the press trip. The idea of an all-expenses paid trip taken at your leisure where you are in charge of where you go and when is, unfortunately for the journalist at least, long gone. It is more likely that the travel company that has coughed up for your trip (there's no such thing as a free lunch) wants to get as much out of you as possible by taking you around as many hotels and restaurants in the area as they can. You are usually on their itinerary and that can be pretty gruelling and limiting – it is in reality a job like any other.

In the interview below, Simon Calder gives an example of how not to pitch to an editor if you are lucky enough to have secured a press trip. Even if you have the trip in the bag, you will still need to work on an angle for a story.

So now you are faced with some of the realities of travel journalism, don't ditch the dream – just be prepared for some hard work.

Travel writing exercise

Real Travel is a real magazine (no pun intended) and, as an exercise, I suggest trying your hand at these two columns that they run. If you think you have done a good job you could even try approaching the editor. (Be warned: he is very busy, and contacting him doesn't guarantee a reply but, as always, it is worth a shot.)

Have you ever? (450 words)
This section is all about sharing a specific experience with other travellers. Your piece needs to be a snippet of your travels, a moment that sticks in your mind that sums up a place, memory or time when you were visiting a country overseas. It could be about something you ate, something you saw, an atmosphere, a place, an amusing story, someone you met along the way. In 450 words sum up a moment such as this – recreate the mood, atmosphere and what you felt. Include details of all your sensory impressions, transporting readers to the scene and encouraging them to follow in your footsteps.

My favourite book (250 words)
Pick out a book that has inspired you to travel – whether it's simply set in a foreign country which you've wanted to visit ever since, or whether it tells of someone's journey and makes the idea and romance of travel appealing. It could be a classic, a new release, fiction or non-fiction. It might be a photography book that includes nothing more than images… Tell your reader a little about why you love the book so much and how it has encouraged your dreams of travelling.

For further information, visit www.realtravelmag.com

Interview: **Simon Calder**

Simon Calder reveals what editors look for in freelance journalists and dispels some of the myths about travel writing.

Simon Calder became travel editor for the *Independent* in 1994. Soon afterwards he began presenting for BBC2's *Travel Show*. In 2003 he became a regular presenter for the *Holiday* programme on BBC1, and in 2007 presented the last film in the final programme of the series, which had run for 37 years. He now presents *Simon Calder's Travel Clinic* on London's news station, LBC 97.3, and contributes regularly to BBC Breakfast News and GMTV. He also shoots a weekly travel blog for Sky.com.

www.simoncalder.com

You weren't always a travel writer were you?
No, and I would urge anyone in these difficult times not to give up the day job. I was working for 15 years before I got a permanent job on a newspaper. Until everything sorts itself it would be madness to try and make a job out of travel journalism. There is an oversupply of people wanting to do the job, and for all the right reasons.

Don't get me wrong, I am fully committed to giving everyone a chance but ultimately it is a very difficult market. If you have to make choices with budgets, as I do, you go with people you know will deliver good quality work and on time, etc. Unfortunately that means there is little space for encouraging new writers – not that I don't want to, it is just a matter of practicalities.

How did you become involved in this profession yourself?
I was a mathematician and an engineer, but I just liked travelling and realised that if you could write about it you could feed your habit.

I have never calculated the number of people who make a living from travel writing but I would imagine it is in the dozens, a very small number. A lot of people we have writing for us have completely other lives as well, away from journalism. It isn't just in journalism that people are doing a bit of this and a bit of that.

Are there any writers that inspired you?
(Laughs) I am not a brilliant consumer of travel books – I rarely get a chance to enjoy reading something. I am more of a writer than a reader.

What advice do you give people who ask you, 'How do I become a travel writer?'
One answer is not to become a travel writer, it is simply not a life I would have considered myself. But being a supplier of travel journalism is a better aspiration.

You need to understand the market and respond to it. Pick up *The Independent Traveller* and it has the same format every week. We have a section called 'Warning of the week' and we hardly get any requests for stories for it. Yet I will get three, already written 10,000-word stories on Uzbekistan! – which I can never get through.

I haven't got the time or inclination to read through a 10,000-word article to see what can be used. But I have got the time to read a three-line pitch. I will say though that we are focusing on our stable of freelancers and it is only natural to protect them in these difficult times.

But there is always scope for something new. The only thing that I can do is try to turn out the best travel section I can with the resources I have.

Is the trick for travel journalists to find new angles or places?
Like every other human being, I love a good story, so that could be based around an event or a place.

An example of someone doing it wrong happened today. Someone called me, bearing in mind it is deadline day, and said 'I have been offered a press trip to France and I am going here, here and here.

Would you like a story?' As politely as I could I said, 'You might want to consider what kind of story you would like to write and then send me an email.'

You clearly love your job – how do you maintain your enthusiasm?

Anyone who is lucky enough to be working in travel journalism, and I will stress journalism, as it is designed to be read on Saturday and thrown away on Sunday, can't help but be overawed by the possibilities and opportunities on offer.

Is it still possible to make a living as a freelance travel journalist?

The freelance travel journalist is appallingly rewarded but the traveller won't care as they will accept the uncertainties that life can deliver.

Do you have any final advice for aspiring travel journalists?

Don't limit your dreams and aspirations. Always focus, focus, focus on those miserable so-and-so's stuck in offices while you are away in Barcelona.

Also, you don't need to be brilliant but you need to be competent. You need to be reliable and know a good story. And if you have those skills, life is never going to be easy, but you stand a very good chance of getting a foot in the door.

Recommended reading: *Lonely Planet Guide to Travel Writing* by David Else, Don George, Charlotte Hindle (Lonely Planet) ISBN: 978-0864427427

8

Lifestyle writing

Definition

Lifestyle writing isn't strictly a 'type' of writing, but a lot of journalism students say that it is something they want to write about. At its widest, it could be said to cover fashion, style, design and other consumer choices such as eating out and shopping.

Lifestyle writing can be found right through the printed media and there are many magazines directed solely at specific lifestyle niches. These might be specific magazines about interiors, for example, or simply a section of a weekend supplement.

As in other areas of journalism, finding one or two specialisms is going to help you focus on what you write about. In addition to the areas mentioned in the 'Definition', we can add entertainment, celebrity, arts, human interest, sex, relationships and health. This sounds like the content you might expect to find in magazines aimed at female readers.

WOMEN'S MAGAZINES

I don't wish to suggest that all women's magazines are concerned only with lifestyle issues; they clearly cover a wider ground than that. But, equally, women make up the largest consumer group of magazines, so presumably the biggest area of opportunities for lifestyle journalists is within women's magazines.

The women's market is fiercely contested and most of the titles are owned by the big publishing houses. Women's magazines have been around since the 17th century and the traditional fare of home and family has been shaken up over the decades so that now you can find a mix of real life stories, fashion, beauty, food, home and travel.

The best way to gauge the dominance of the women's market (and look for some potential magazines to work for) is to browse the magazine section of your local newsagent or supermarket. The shelves strain under their weight.

HUMAN INTEREST

A staple element of journalism is to look for the human interest angle to a story. Take a large subject, such as cancer. There are lots of statistics about cancer. A quick look on the Cancer Research UK website (www.cancerresearchuk.org) tells me that there are 26 commonly-diagnosed types of cancer and 293,601 people were diagnosed with cancer during 2006 in the UK.

Although these statistics are shocking, they are still just statistics that can be shrugged off. However, what if I introduce you to Sarah, a young mother with three children who are all under the age of eight. If you could see a photo of them all together and see how normal she looks, you would realise that she could be your friend, neighbour or someone you work with. 'The worst thing,' she says 'is knowing I won't see my kids grow up.'

Human interest helps make a story real so a common tactic used by journalists is to frame a story around an individual's story. If the article looks at how cancer rates have risen in the last 25 years, introducing the reader to Sarah, going on to explain the statistics and then rounding off with a bit more of Sarah's story makes a nicely-rounded piece.

Deadlines

A factor worth noting is that women's magazines often work one season ahead, reflecting the fashion industry with which they work closely. They will also plan their editions several months in advance. So if you are thinking of pitching them a story with a Christmas theme, you need to get in there early on, even as early as September.

LOCAL LIFESTYLE

Chapter 18 'Understanding the Media Landscape' will identify how to approach researching opportunities in your local area. This is important because most of the journalists working on the glossy magazines who get to interview all the celebs would have spent some time in the less glamorous surroundings of their local newspaper or local what's on guide.

I can think of three or four magazines that are local to me that produce a high percentage of lifestyle content. Some of it isn't so glamorous – a profile of a dentists or a preview of a local theatre production if you are lucky – but writing for such magazines will show you the ropes and help you to develop a portfolio which could prove to a *Vogue* editor that you can string a sentence together on any subject.

It also gets you out there and working as a journalist. As Damian Barr says in the following interview, 'You need to be out there travelling, eating, drinking, shopping, reading, going to the theatre and going to weird places on and off the beaten track.'

Also, working on a local magazine will make you appreciate those film premiers all the more when you do finally get there.

FASHION – KNOW YOUR STUFF

Hopefully, the reason you want to write about fashion is because you are already a fashion junky. Turning your passions into a career is a great move. However, keep pushing yourself to learn new things. Knowing which brands are cool and those which aren't won't be enough to keep you going forever. Learn about the industry and what makes it tick. Find out about the people behind the scenes.

If you are dreaming of covering fashion shows but still working at Top Shop, remember that this might give you a head start over your competitors as you are face-to-face with consumers and you know what they are buying right now. Learn about supply chains and what has influenced the designs that are selling. What isn't selling? Why is that?

Journalists are people who ask questions and that holds firm in whatever niche of journalism you work in.

Lifestyle writing exercise

Think about the audience you are targeting and then write 500 words on a new trend that you have spotted.

Read the following interview with Damian Barr in which he suggests that trends are always coming and going. Here are some ideas to help you begin:

- Have you noticed a trend that is particular to your area or your group of friends?

- Is there some other trend that has caught your attention? For example, are people starting to wear new combinations?

- Is the increase in the number of street parties symptomatic of a greater desire to connect with our neighbours?

- Have students changed in any way since the credit crunch because they are less likely to find a job when they graduate?

TRAINING

- MA Fashion and Lifestyle Journalism: 1 year full-time, 2 years part-time at University for the Creative Arts (UCA), Epsom, www.ucreative.ac.uk

- PG Cert. in Fashion: Fashion and Lifestyle Journalism, London College of Fashion at University of Arts London, www.arts. ac.uk

Interview: **Damian Barr**

Damian Barr reveals what
it takes to be a lifestyle
journalist.

Damian Barr is a writer,
journalist and playwright.
His witty-but-weighty
lifestyle and social trends features appear in *The Times* and
the *Telegraph* as well as magazines like *Olive*, *Country Life* and
Harpers. Radio Four has now broadcast two of his plays and he is
co-writing a third. He has been short-listed for a prestigious British
Press Award and, most recently, for an Arts & Business Award
for his Reader in Residence project at the Andaz Hotel. *Get It
Together: Survive Your Quarterlife Crisis* was his first book. He also
hosts a regular Literary Salon for Soho and Shoreditch Houses.

**You are described on *The Times*'s website as being 'dedicated to
discovering new lifestyle and social trends, people or places'. So,
I guess you have your finger on the pulse?**

I certainly do! I have been on the CoolBrands Council for the last
three years and I am talking to a number of weekend supplements
about doing a column called 'On Trend'.

So what is new right now?
Well, in restaurants there is a move to being cashless so all
transactions take place with a card that says you belong to the
restaurant and you swipe your card and the whole process is
much faster.

There is also a move to lots of smaller tapas-style plates during
these recessionary times. People don't want to commit and it
is also part of our cultural ADHD. We have a kind of media
tapas thing going on where people consume small snippets of
information.

Can you explain a bit about lifestyle writing and what it entails?
As a lifestyle journalist, you are looking at the way people live
their lives. You need to be out there travelling, eating, drinking,
shopping, reading, going to the theatre, going to weird places *on*
and *off* the beaten track. You can't be a lifestyle journalist and work
in an office, unless you like just recycling press releases.

Lifestyle writing can be perceived to be quite fluffy and
nonsensical but it is actually underpinned by quite serious cultural
trends. My degree is in English and Sociology and my Masters is in
Sociology, so I am coming at it from that background.

What was your own route into journalism?
The Times came to my university and I got work experience on a
student magazine they were producing. I was then the editor of
that magazine for a year. They closed it down and so I went and
did more hard news stuff for the *Independent* that lasted a year or
so, and then *The Times* tempted me back with a new magazine
about work that they were launching. The paper then asked me to
do a column about graduates' work experiences and that became
my book, *Quarterlife Crisis*.

So many students start on student magazines and I would
recommend that to anyone. I had work experience on my local
paper before all this and I had a year abroad and worked on a
paper then too. You can make all your mistakes there.

I actually dropped out of my journalism degree after the first
year as I didn't find it very intellectually stimulating – I got my
shorthand and failed my media law. I would always suggest taking
the job over the qualification.

How has your work outside of journalism come about?
Journalism is my bread and butter but I also work with the
CoolBrands Council, and do some consultancy work. People are
buying into my marketable skills and the most important thing
in a recession is to be working. I don't work in PR but I know
journalists that do.

It is very easy to move from journalism into PR rather than the other way round. I have a good relationship with PRs. God knows in lifestyle, a newspaper isn't going to pay for a trip to Chile but a PR company will. So you have to work with PR if it is going to open doors.

Do you think freelancing is a lifestyle choice? Is it becoming more normal?
I think people are having it imposed on them by the recession – a lot of staff writers are having it foisted upon them by losing their jobs. They may have been journalists for a long time but they are like a fish out of water when it comes to freelancing and having to pitch ideas and that sort of stuff. Some are making the transition better than others, obviously.

But generally portfolio working is on the rise. All the other things I do – presenting, playwriting, etc. – are things that lead me to more stories. After a while it all becomes self-perpetuating.

You have also written a book and plays for Radio 4. Did being a journalist help with that?
In all honesty, I was writing a novel and I gave it to a friend of mine who is a novelist, Laura Lockington. She said it was dire and told me that I write conversation like a journalist: 'You report it, you don't imagine it', and she was right! So we started working on it and another friend, Julie Burchill, popped round and saw what we were doing and she liked it and passed it on to a producer friend of hers. So that is how it happened.

But writing plays was *so* difficult. As a journalist, you are used to economy of expression – saying as much as possible in as few words as possible. Will Self calls writing in different styles 'code switching' and it is much more difficult than you would imagine.

[At this point there is the sound of clucking from Damian's chickens.]
Is it true that you work from a shed in your garden?
I love my shed – it is great. I used to work in a spare room and what I wanted to do was to close a door on my work. I have got a swanky shed, with heating and a wireless connection and it has

better flooring than in my house. It also doubles up as a spare room when people come and stay, and as a bar in the summer! I definitely think it is good to have boundaries as much as you can.

Finally, do you have any other advice for aspiring journalists?
You have to be writing all the time and showing your writing to people. I can't bear preciousness. If an editor calls you at 10 am and wants copy by 2 pm, you have to just get it done. And sometimes getting it done is the best you can do, so you just have to get on with it.

Also journalists need to get out because that is where stories happen. You don't spend your life writing – if you just want to write, become a novelist.

And a freelancer is also an accountant, administrator and the IT person, so you have to be prepared to be multi-functional.

In lifestyle journalism, so much is based on your viewpoint and people will criticise you for that. So you have to be thick-skinned. You also have to develop a clear viewpoint and not be afraid to express it.

Interview: **Lia Leendertz**

Lia Leendertz writes about gardening for the *Guardian*'s *Weekend* magazine, while also being mother to two small children, keeping on top of her allotment and writing horticulture books.

How did you become a freelance journalist?
I studied horticulture at college and then got a job as a trainee horticulture journalist at a magazine called *The Garden*, which is the Royal Horticultural Society's magazine. That was a year's training. Then I worked at *Horticulture Week* and then I went back to *The Garden* before going freelance.

I might have just gone into a more practical form of gardening had the opportunity at *The Garden* not come up. Part of the reason I went freelance was that I wanted to move back to my home town of Bristol.

What was it like going from being a staff writer to being freelance?
It was taking a leap, I knew there were people on two magazines that I could do some stuff for. I was really hoping it would be okay, but it was just a case of getting a computer and starting.

How did your column in the *Guardian* come about?
It happened within about a year of being freelance. It was a very flukey process of knowing the right person in the right place. I had a friend who studied at Kew and who was also a journalist I had worked with at *Horticulture Week*. Kim Wilde used to write the column for the *Guardian* and they wanted another female to sit alongside Christopher Lloyd.

It was my ideal job as I had always read the magazine. I had to submit a column and answer some questions and then I got the job! I think I had an advantage, as I was such a fan already. That was six years ago.

I still occasionally get some work from some other magazines, such as *Gardens Illustrated*, which is really nice as that was one of the magazines I have always really liked and aspired to write for.

Are your books a result of your links with the *Guardian*?
I have four out now. I think my RHS connections from *The Garden* have helped me most.

Was your initial interest in writing or horticulture?
Horticulture in a way, but I always enjoyed writing at school. I had a few years of not knowing what to do and it was during that period that I discovered gardening. One of my mum's friends said, 'You know you can study gardening, don't you?' and I thought, 'Oh right' and went and did that. But it did feel very natural to write about it, as well as doing it.

How does being freelance fit in with your parenting commitments?
It is really good in the sense that I can work from home, work part-time and work around things. The bad side is that I don't get to get away from the house and share in things with colleagues.

How do you structure your work?
I have two days of definite childcare a week from relatives, sometimes a third. On the other days I really try and switch off and not check emails and stuff, as I know I have a better time with the kids if I don't. I used to split the days when the kids were younger, but I have changed that recently and now try and spend a solid five days with them. My aim is to separate the two parts of my life but it doesn't always work out like that.

Would you go back into an office now if someone were to offer it to you?
I don't know, maybe when the kids are older. It crosses my mind, but it would have to be a pretty good offer!

How difficult is it juggling parenthood and a career?
In the run up to having my first child I had to work really hard to get six weeks ahead in my columns. I met all these other women who were enjoying six months maternity leave. Then once I had her, I had to get back to it after those six weeks. So I was working upstairs and popping downstairs to breastfeed – I felt quite sorry for myself at that point!

Do you have any pearls of wisdom for an aspiring journalist?
I would suggest people work on a magazine or a newspaper before trying to freelance. But the things I have always stuck by is getting working in on time and getting it in on word count. It sounds so basic, but so many writers don't do that. Also your editor knows they aren't dealing with a prima donna.

I have been very lucky in my career. I have had so many ideas rejected but always managed to find some work. I have had my head in my hands on many an occasion.

Would you encourage your kids to go into journalism?
There has been a huge spike in lifestyle writers from the 1980s
onward, so it is a relatively new phenomenon. Maybe the internet
will have put paid to that by the time they are starting their
careers, but I think I would encourage them into journalism as it is
a pretty nice life overall.

9

Sports writing

Definition

Sports writing incorporates many styles of journalism including match reports, profiles of and interviews with sporting stars, news, opinion and even scandalous gossip with no foundation in truth!

There is an incredible number of sports magazines, newspaper supplements, websites and blogs – sports writing could command a book of its own. Predictably there is more content aimed at football fans, as well as more websites and magazines. But then, there are also more people wanting to write about football as opposed to water polo for example.

As for aspiring sports writers, the advice seems to be to start local and find areas that aren't being covered by other writers. Consider writing reports on your local cricket club, local table tennis league, school matches, etc. This will give you the time to develop and the opportunity to find out whether this is something that you want to pursue and invest more heavily in. If you are already involved in local sports, writing reports will give you greater purpose and an opportunity to introduce yourself to local sports people. You never know, catch a rising star and you might have made one of the most important contacts of your career.

HOW TO WRITE A MATCH REPORT

We have already established that if you follow the 'who, what, where, when, how and why' formula, you are well on your way to becoming a journalist. Well, this is certainly true in writing a match report. At the very least, the reader will want to know:

- what the score was;

- who played well;

- what the decisive moments were;

- how the teams responded to the challenge;

- when the next match takes place.

Again, remember the golden rule: 'Who is the audience?' If you are writing a local report for the golf club's newsletter, you will of course include the score; but also write about the atmosphere – was the young challenger to the existing cup holder fiercely contested or was it a friendly affair? Think about why the reader should care about it. Was it the most important warm-up event before something else takes place? If it was a local half marathon, for instance, was there anyone running it who is going on to the London marathon?

As with all other types of journalism, go and chat to people. See if the other spectators saw events in the same way you did – someone might offer a nugget of information that you didn't know about. The scorer is just back from injury, the team make extra cash by working as male strippers. Bingo, you just found yourself another story.

BLOGS

There are lots of blogs for teams these days and writing one could offer you a way in. Blogs aren't the easy answer for finding an audience that people sometimes think they are going to be as getting readers for your blog is always a challenge.

Contributing to other people's blogs might offer a better solution. You are unlikely to be paid, but it gets you used to producing content to a brief and means you maintain the freedom to write for lots of people.

PHOTO TIPS

Don't forget that photographs can cement your article getting published. The quality doesn't have to be amazing, but try to frame your photos well and make sure they are in focus and not blurred. Look out for drama, movement and decisive moments such as:

- a good tackle;
- two players going for the same ball;
- the moment a striker hits the ball;
- the celebration.

Sports writing exercise

As sports writer Andy Sloan suggests in the following interview, one of the best ways to start is to go out and report on something that is happening in your locality. So for this exercise, do exactly that. Go to a local amateur football match, rugby match or kids' netball game and write up what you see. It might not get published, but I bet it would be great fun and the team themselves and the one man and his dog that support them will be interested in reading it.

Looking through my local paper, there is a short match report of a netball game which is 100 words and includes a list of the names in the teams. It also includes the result and states that the teams were in division five of the local netball league. There is a slightly bigger piece on a girls' hockey team from a local school that won an under-12s regional tournament. There is a picture of the girls with their medals and trophy. The piece is 300 words and it describes the match, says how many teams were in the tournament and includes a few quotes from the PE teacher who coached the team.

Try doing something similar to the above stories, depending on what you can find to write about. Don't forget to add a catchy headline.

Further reading

Martin Samuel of *The Times* has been Sports Journalists' Association Sports Writer of the Year for three consecutive years (2006–08) at the British Sports Journalism Awards. For further information, visit: www.sportsjournalists.co.uk

Interview: **Andy Sloan**

Changing careers is increasingly common, and journalism is a career that can offer opportunities to people trained in other disciplines.

30-year-old Andy Sloan describes himself as an 'Internet Reporter/ Sports Writer/Internet Sports Writer' for Bristol's *Evening Post*, but it wasn't always this way. As a law student, he decided that he would travel from London to South East Asia overland carrying a football table. He wrote about his adventures in the hilarious *23 Sweet FAs: Round the World with a Football Table* (Virgin Books). He continued with his law career but found the lure of sports writing too great to ignore.

What was your 'first career' Andy?

I went into law straight in from uni, then law school and then onto a graduate training scheme at a massive law firm in the City. But I knew as soon as I started the graduate training scheme that I didn't want to do it.

Why did you want to change?

I knew that I needed to change when my weekend would get cancelled and I'd be sat with boxes and boxes of files. I got some good training which would apply to any profession, but when you wake up with a feeling of dread or boredom, you know you can't do it for the rest of your life.

It was always going to be sports writing for me, as sport is my first love. I had my book published in 2006, which was my main catalyst in changing careers.

So how did you make the transition from law to sports journalism?

Besides the book, I spent my holidays doing work experience at various newspapers such as the local paper in Norwich and the Euro Sport website. It was difficult juggling the two jobs but I got some good names down on my CV. I was aiming to get to a position where my law career was half-way down my CV. I wanted to show that I was committed and understood what the sector was like.

So you had a long-term plan?

Yes and no. The book was the main thing, but I also spoke to as many people as possible, mates of mates, and they recommended doing a course. Not just to gain the skills, as you can do much of that yourself, but it was about the contacts and the alumni that you meet. I fancied going back to study anyway, and was lucky that the law had paid sufficiently for me to make that choice.

Is there anything else the course gave you?

Shorthand. I can now put notes on the fridge that the wife can't understand! It also saves so much time in transcription. Other than that, it was tightening up the writing, presenting ideas, just hammering in the basics really.

And you got a job on the *Evening Post* shortly after graduating?

Yes, I was lucky. But I had done a two-week work placement that I had arranged myself. I worked really hard during that and got a few bits and pieces afterwards such as covering the odd event, which kept me in touch with the editor. Some of this I did for free and some was paid. Then finally a job came up and I got a call saying to apply, and I got the job.

Do you have advice for anyone else wanting to make a similar transition?

I think it is to just make things happen for yourself – if you don't make calls no-one will call you. I believe in that old Gary Player quote, 'You make your own luck'. It was the same with my book. I wrote it and then got a publisher by banging on doors.

Looking back, was it a difficult process?

It was easy in the sense of knowing what I wanted to do, but the decision to move was hard. Handing in my resignation to my old job was nerve wracking but it was a weight off my shoulders.

Are there any downsides to being a sports journalist?

The one drawback is this job starts far too early: 7–7.30. I should leave at 3.30–4 but keep staying late!

Do you have any sports writing tips?

Just start by writing something. It might sound stupid, but do a match report on your son's football match and get it in the newsletter. I know someone who wrote reports on his golf club's matches, and his local newspaper has just started printing them. He is retired and is starting a new career and building up a pile of cuttings.

What future plans do you have?

Maybe freelancing and writing books. For me, in starting out I wanted to get the experience, gain some confidence.

10

Music journalism

Definition

Music journalism is obviously writing about music, but the two main types of writing styles that tend to be published are interview-led features (of bands, individuals or people connected to the music business) or reviews of new events (such as gigs, CDs, DVDs, books and-increasingly-online broadcasts).

STARTING POINT

Music is a starting point for many journalists. Stuart Maconie and Andrew Collins, for example, both started at the *NME* and now write for the highest-selling weekly magazine in the UK, the *Radio Times*.

Music writing of course appeals to many young people because young people like music. The glamour is appealing, as is getting into gigs for free, receiving free CDs for review, having PR people phone you up trying to foist freebies on you. Meeting lots of musicians and getting 'Access All Areas' badges. Being friends with musicians, becoming part of the circle of trust and getting invited to do exclusive interviews and write their official biography. Becoming the 'fifth member of the band' that keeps it all together. Okay, maybe that is going a bit far.

Writing about music isn't a passport to the riches and fame that musicians can, in increasingly rarer instances, experience. Music journalism is one of the worst paid areas of journalism, mainly because there are so many people wanting to do it for free. Having said that, however, older editors will allow opportunities for younger writers, and proving yourself in this area can open doors in other areas of journalism as time progresses.

LEARNING TO TAME THE PASSION

A classic problem that editors see over and over again in young writers is their passion about certain artists but blindness to the merits of others. Say you are a metal fan, trying to write a review about the latest urban tune. There are a couple of options. Either write for a niche publication such as *Metal Hammer* which isn't going anywhere near stuff out of its covered genres anyway (readers of this magazine would also share and appreciate your passion so you are on safe ground), or learn to temper your passions and write in a slightly more broad-minded fashion that suits your editor's brief. The latter would secure you more work, but inevitably involves some compromise.

'Criticism isn't about how you feel about something, but why you feel that way', wrote the *Guardian*'s music writer Alexis Petridis in an advice column for aspiring music journalists (see Further Reading below).

AVOIDING CLICHÉS

There are so many clichés in music writing that you could write an entire review made up of them. Check this out:

> As the band took the stage the atmosphere was electric. The hairs stood up on the back of my neck as Johnny bashed out those well-known opening chords to 'Smells like Bullshit'. The crowd went mental. The band delighted us with hit after hit and we all sang along, we knew all the words. They are such legends. The drummer drummed and the bass player strummed in perfect unison. I nearly wet myself. If you haven't heard them yet, you must do so now. They rock.

Okay, I am exaggerating for the sake of effect. But there is a serious point here: by avoiding clichés you will be taken more seriously by readers. If you are a massive fan of a band, try and assess their performance a little more objectively. Was it a good show in relation to the rest of the tour? Are they a good live act or are they a bit wooden? Did they give value for money?

COMMISSIONS

The kinds of writing you might be commissioned to produce are CD and gig reviews (also refer to Chapter 3 'Writing Reviews') and features about artists including interviews, which are often a very exciting prospect for a new writer.

In reality, interviews may involve visiting hotels, to be escorted through and given an 'allocation' with an artist, while the PR person sullenly stands there listening to the interview and even butting in if they feel you are straying into territory that their client isn't comfortable with. The other more likely situation is the 'phoner', which is a similar scenario but conducted over the phone. A PR will call you at the allotted time and will put you through to the tired and emotional artist who has already been asked the same questions by several other journalists. The PR stays on the line, listening to your interview, and can butt in if you ask any questions likely to upset the artist. They will also tell you when your allotted time slot is up.

For these kinds of interviews, I suggest you work extra hard to ask your subject a few interesting questions to stop them dropping off and giving you their rehearsed schpiel. Also, it is probably not a good idea to keep your killer question until last just in case you do get cut short. Hopefully, the PR person will be able to provide you with biographies and so on before your call, so you don't need to ask during the interview for information that you can research yourself.

OTHER AREAS FOR MUSIC WRITERS

There is a large market in music magazines that focus on instruments, and writing reviews of guitars or comparing new amps and gadgets or music software can be lucrative. It is easier to write about this material if you are a musician but I have met journalists who can't play a note and have written about it. Remember that a good writer can write about anything, but you have to weigh up how much time it takes to cram in a load of new information. Time is money and only you can decide how much money your time is worth.

As already mentioned, the bad news is that music journalism doesn't pay very well. There are many reasons for this, but a big part of it is that there are many young people trying to make a name for themselves and working for free. There are more music magazines, websites, e-zines and the like than ever before and less and less advertising revenue from the music industry.

NAVIGATING MUSIC INDUSTRY AND MAGAZINE CHANGES

The music industry is experiencing a similar future shock to journalism; the technology to share and distribute music free of charge is taking away the old financial certainties that have always supported the big companies. Phil Sutcliffe talks about this in the following interview.

A side effect of the changes in the music industry is that the only growth area within music publishing is in what marketing people call 'heritage titles'. These are magazines such as *Mojo* and *The Word*, which are pitched at one of the few groups of people still buying CDs – the male aged 40+ market. As many established journalists such as Phil Sutcliffe are working for these magazines, you will meet some stiff competition when pitching for feature writing. But, as he suggests, there are other routes which include writing CD reviews or being able to exploit a unique contact that you may have fostered.

So if your dream is to work for the *NME*, start with a freebie, a local publication, your own blog. Much of the music business is 'who you know' over anything else, which is another reason why this is an ideal area of journalism for young people who already know others in bands and can build on that trust. An outsider with a huge age gap might find it difficult to make the contacts needed – not to mention staying up to the small hours to bag an interview.

Music writing exercises

Write a 150-word review of the last CD you bought.

Write a 150-word review of the last gig that you saw.

Go and see a local band and after the gig ask if you can interview them. Be prepared with half a dozen questions – do some research beforehand and see if there is a blog or website that is focused on your local music scene. If there isn't, perhaps you are the person to start one. Also check out the band's MySpace page to see if there's anything that you can pick up on for your interview:

- What do they do for day jobs?

- Where did they all meet?

- Are they really influenced by children television theme tunes or are they just making that up?

Before you rush off to do the interview, re-read the interviewing techniques included in Chapter 6.

Further reading

- Advice from the *Guardian*'s music writer Alex Petredis:

  http://arts.guardian.co.uk/youngcritics/story/0,,2289650,00. html#article_continue

- www.rocksbackpages.com has classic articles from all the legendary music writers down the years

Interview: **Phil Sutcliffe**

Phil Sutcliffe has been a journalist for 40 years and 30 of those have been dedicated to music freelancing. He was the first music journalist to interview Sting, and has worked for practically every publication of note: *Sounds*, *Melody Maker*, *Q*, *The Face* and *MOJO*. He also teaches two training courses at the NUJ: 'So you wanna be a rock writer?' and 'Pitch and deal for freelancers'.

Are you working on anything interesting at the moment?
Yes, a piece on Woody Guthrie for *MOJO* which is proving very difficult. Luckily it has been put back a month. It is heading to 7,000 words but needs to be 4,000. I will have to approach it after my holiday with a fresh mind.

How did your career start?
I started as a graduate apprentice in Newcastle. And for the last two years of that employment at the *Newcastle Chronicle* I was applying for my next job. I got rejected by 174 prospective employers. Every one of them was a journalism job, about 50 of which were for the BBC. I had ten interviews, but I was unemployable apparently. So eventually I just went freelance in Newcastle, rather sooner than I had intended.

I started freelancing for local media, which paid very poorly then as it does now. Very few freelancers can exclusively make a living out of local media. I started contacting the dailies as well as the weeklies.

Did you have a specific niche?
My niche was covering gigs in Newcastle, and the trend then was that many national tours would start in the North East. So I had

this little advantage and did a lot of live reviews. I swiftly had to choose sides between rival publications and *Sounds* was the one which I did the most for.

Is it true that you used several pseudonyms?

Yes I did. There is a lot of competition between publications so pseudonyms mean you can work for rival publications. In the 80s I had three pseudonyms as this was a boom period for publications.

Smash Hits and *The Face* asked me to write for them, and I wanted to, so I had to use a nom de plume. It isn't a problem if you just contact the accounts department of the publication you are writing for and let them know; you don't need to involve the editor.

You have been freelance for 30 years. Has this been by choice or necessity?

Oh definitely choice. I started earlier than intended as I mentioned, but I come from a line of self-employed people so perhaps that unconsciously led me that way. It has its ups and downs; for example, my income has fluctuated – receipts have gone from nothing in one month up to £7,000 in another. That has been my lowest and highest and they both came very close together.

You must have seen some dramatic changes over those 30 years?

Probably the biggest changes have been technology driven. I have had very close relationships with editors but the technology has worked against this process, which I will explain in a little more detail.

When I started, you did five carbon copies and hand delivered your copy. The Amstrad years didn't change this process – you took your disc in and you would sit and work through that story with the editor line by line. That was a tremendous pleasure; it improved the quality of journalism and improved the page and what the reader consumed, and it would also improve your ability as a writer.

It was email that killed this process. I haven't been into the *Mojo* office, full of people I know, for a month. And that means the attention to detail may start to fade. And you might not be at the forefront of their minds any more. At *Mojo* we are doing everything by email and the dynamic of conversation is slowed down by email communication. It is more remote and we don't work as a team.

I think most people enjoy co-operative creativity and the freelancer is more and more a lone wolf. The technology has increased the isolation.

Did you learn anything else by working closely with editors like this?
Nowadays many of the editorial roles have become management roles and, like I said, I have been lucky in working with many great editors. But that experience is becoming less and less common.

I also hear journalists complain that their work gets 'interfered with'. I wonder, 'Well, what is going on here? Do you think every word you write is perfect? Can you listen to criticism?'! I think there are many ways in which to write an article and there is no right or wrong way. I would encourage writers to be open-minded.

What about the nuts and bolts of music writing? How does it differ from other journalism?
There are always different shades of objectivity, but especially in any criticism or cultural work. Music writing is the same as any type of criticism and on the course that I teach we look at two reviews. In one, the journalist is saying 'I, I, I, I' all the time and that is the fundamental thing that has an effect on all writing.

I have habitually used objective techniques but didn't during the *Sounds* days. It was *Q* that established it in opposition to the 60s' style of New Journalism. This was a hippy idea that there was no such thing as objectivity, so it was okay to put yourself in as it is being honest. Lester Bangs is one of the gods of this. And most untrained journalists, which many music journalists are, embraced this. The rule on *Q* was 'you can say "fuck" but you can't say "I"'. They wanted you to look at the subject rather than bring attention to the writer. I loved that idea and embraced that.

I don't claim to be absolutely objective but you can express yourself objectively and give reasons for what you say.

Some people can bypass all this and land themselves a £150,000-a-year column on a national newspaper but, for the rest of us working stiffs, knowing how to write is very important!

Is there anything else that people new to writing need to know about?
I'd say planning. My present problems are due to lack of planning, which leads to a lack of analysis.

All it says is that this work isn't easy. Working at the top of our individual ability is always going to be difficult. I could have done with an hour with the editor, but the way things are I have to solve this problem myself.

Presumably changes in the music business are impacting on the careers of music journalists?
The shit of it is that making a living is increasing limited; it really is receding. We have a wonderful combination of short-term and long-term crisis. The long-term one is the music industry's crisis which has transferred itself into the music media, as the business went into decline there was less money to advertise.

Plus there is a proliferation of unpaid amateur publications. Music journalists are offering themselves as the skivvy of the economy, which is a natural trend in capitalism. It may well be that the media is part of a widespread trend towards not paying people. Most of the workers are going to be hobbyists, so young people need to look seriously at this and decide how they are going to make it work.

It is the mid-career people who are suffering the worst; it basically means you need to do something else to make your money.

A prime example of how things have changed is *Clash* magazine. It doesn't pay people to write! And it sits on the shelf next door to *Mojo*, which pays £300 for 1,000 words. That is the business behind the journalism.

Journalism remains a fine means of expression, but young journalists will clearly have to think twice about it as a career.

Do you have any final tips for aspiring journalists?
Live music is doing very well, so live reviews are still strong. But CD reviews are the mainstay for aspiring journalists as they run 100 to 150 a month. It is a crowded market, but journalists need to look around them and search what assets they have for developing a niche. Diversify is a key word: develop ten specialisms. You can't just rely on your enthusiasm in this business. I have been a journalist for 30 years and this is the worst time I have seen in that time. It is a bastard out there!

11

Finding ideas

Ideas are the lifeblood of the freelance journalist. A staff writer is lucky in the sense that they are part of an editorial team, which might have a meeting once a week to discuss ideas for upcoming editorial content. The staff writer will then be designated a story and told to go to work.

The freelancer has to have their own meeting with themselves and bounce ideas off of themselves!

SYNERGY

Books on creative thinking suggest that ideas are easier to generate in groups – a process which is called 'synergy'. For example, I might suggest doing a feature on social networking. 'It's been done,' you might respond. Rethinking off the cuff might lead me to think, 'Okay, how about social networking marriages? People who meet their partners on Facebook?' And this might be an angle that can be pitched to a magazine.

If you get to a stage where you have a good relationship with an editor, you might be lucky enough to find that you have a synergistic relationship with them (if they have the time and the inclination). But let's assume that you are sitting at home, head in hand and staring out the window. This scenario shouldn't be too difficult for a freelance journalist to imagine!

READ AND RECYCLE

There are very few, purely original ideas. Many ideas are triggered by something else, so read everything and don't be afraid to put your own angle on things you see elsewhere. For example, a local newspaper might do a story about a local vintage car club raising money with a sponsored drive from London to Brighton, which could be re-angled for a magazine on vintage cars.

Another classic technique is seeing a small part of another article and exploring it further. So in the vintage car piece someone interviewed might say, 'We are raising money for this charity because they helped me when I broke every bone in my body last year.' Cue your 'Man comes back from the dead' story for a gossip magazine.

Reading NiBs ('News in Brief' columns: see Appendix 1, Jargon buster) is a great place to find something that can be explored in greater detail for another publication or in some cases even the same publication.

Reading magazines and newspapers well out of your normal sphere of reading can also help you with this process. Online newspapers generated abroad can help you search for similar things in the UK.

Please note: I am not suggesting you plagiarise anything. You will soon be spotted if you are literally recycling someone else's material, and your reputation counts for a lot in freelancing.

Pieces of writing are often covered by copyright and you are leaving yourself open to being sued if you steal work.

KEEP A NOTEBOOK

Inspiration has to come from somewhere, so read widely and keep a notebook. A notebook is your memory when you are out and about. I sometimes think that writing down ideas allows space for new ones to come through. I have met writers who have been stuck with the one original idea that they had many years ago and have been carrying around ever since. Some of these are great, of course, and will see the light of day eventually, but many won't. And the writer who wants to write for a living (be it part-time or full-time) needs to be able to drop an idea, even if it is good, and move on to the next project.

Good ideas have a way of re-emerging anyway. Timing is often an important factor and sometimes you have to wait for months or even years to get an idea to take off.

BEST IDEAS FOR TOP CLIENTS

I operate a strict 'Best ideas for best clients' policy. 'Best client' could be the organisation paying me the most money, but there is a stronger likelihood that it will be someone who I know would run with the idea. Getting a flow of published pieces is often better than waiting for the people who will pay better because work often leads to new work. I have hit draughts before and found that once I start working on anything, however small or poorly paid, it gets me out of the rut of thinking, 'Oh no, all is doomed'.

HOW LONG TO OFFER AN IDEA TO SOMEONE?

Students often ask me how long they should wait for a response before offering their idea to another publication. I usually allow a weekly paper a week to respond; if they haven't in that timeframe I will take it to the next paper that publishes similar work.

A weekly or monthly magazine might take a little longer. It is good to try and find out how far ahead publications are planning. Women's magazines tend to work three months ahead as they are led by the fashion industry which is always working on next season's clothes.

IGNORE THE SILENCE

Hearing nothing from a publication doesn't mean you should just pack up and move on. I have had commissions from papers that ignored my first three or four emails. Editors or commissioning staff often don't like to write back to lots of freelancers saying 'Not this time thanks', so frequently you will just hit a wall of silence.

People often project their own fears into this silence and assume it means the worse. It doesn't mean anything except that they didn't want that idea at that time. Prepare some more ideas and get pitching – see Chapter 20 'Planning, organisation and time management'.

CREATIVE THINKING TIPS

- Read things outside of your normal remit. Different people have different styles and exposing yourself to them can jog this creative process.

- Think locally/regionally/nationally. Slanting an article to fit your niche is perfectly acceptable – do it before someone else does.

- Update old debates. Think back to articles that made an impression on you in the past. Remember when everyone was scared of the impact of the internet? Well, what technology scares people today? Is it social networking stalkers? Identity theft? Phishing emails?

- Think ahead. Many magazines and newspapers will run articles that are similar every year, say around a special day like Mother's Day. There is often an opportunity here for a freelancer who can think of a new angle on an old subject.

- Think laterally. I once wrote an article on a poet for a literary magazine, and in it he mentioned how writing had helped him with his mental health. So I contacted a mental health magazine and they ran the piece as well. Both paid an average amount but combined they made that article well worth doing.

12

How to approach editors

The roles of 'the editor' vary with the size of the organisation. To reflect this, if you look through vacancies for editors on www. Journalism.co.uk you will see the salary of an editor in a regional magazine or a small niche magazine will be around the £20–25,000 mark, whereas Alan Rusbridger, the editor of the *Guardian*, has a salary of over £450,000. Clearly their roles are very different, but how?

EDITORIAL ROLES

Managing editor

Let's start at the top. Managing the business side of things is a managing editor or publisher. These lucky people stack the figures and will be your saviours if they increase their freelance budget, or the meanies if they cut it.

Often they will represent the editorial voice in meetings with the rest of the business, i.e. advertising and finance. In an ideal world they will be protecting the interests of the reader from people whose more commercial perspective would mean that they would be happy to see magazines made up entirely of adverts.

Publisher

This role can include overseeing several departments, as it was in my case. So, managing editorial (and indirectly freelancers), financial and advertising departments will all be part of the job.

Editor

In the clichéd newspaper role, the editor will have their own office and staff writers will come in and out to be set straight by the firey, cigarette-smoking New Yorker. In 21st century Britain, however, editors are likely to be stressed out, poorly paid, overworked individuals who don't reply to freelancers' emails because they are concentrating on their next deadline.

Features editor

In a larger magazine, where there are sufficient staff to be able to divide the roles, someone will look after the 'management stuff' (see above) and ideally someone else will look after the 'writing stuff'. A good features editor will be someone whom you can speak to regarding your work, what to focus on, what is worth only a mention. They may also 'sub' the piece (see sub-editor) below.

Deputy editor

As the name implies, a deputy will look after the editorial side of things when the editor is taken up by other management demands. They may also have responsibilities such as dealing with freelancers and may also edit or sub-edit copy.

Sub editors

Not a lower sub-species as the name might suggest, but highly-skilled professionals in the fine arts of grammar, media law and creating good-quality readable copy. These are the people who cut and change freelancers' copy, which some freelancers take umbridge at.

Personally, I think having a professional look over your work, improve it and check it for inaccuracies is an absolute blessing. Think of it as a final polish before being set before the public. If you experience drastic changes, it could be worth speaking to them afterwards to see if they can tell you why. The reason a piece is cut may be to do with space rather than poor quality of copy. But if this happens to you repeatedly, you might need to look closer to home and consider what you have learnt from the process.

Other editors

Larger newspapers may break down the role even further to cover their areas of coverage including photo editors, commissioning editors, news editors, sports editors, business editors. The job description, however, is largely the same.

OTHER EDITORIAL CONCERNS

It is worth knowing what other things an editor might be facing when they are not editing your copy or commissioning your work. Largely their job description would include some of the following:

- Guardian of the publication's brand, making sure that all content is appropriate to the brand.

- Guiding staff writers and freelancers in producing content for the publication. This may or may not be in consultation with other members of staff and departments.

- Thinking of new columns, sections, etc. and ditching old ones that aren't working out.

- Ultimately responsible for circulation (with distribution managers). It is often the editor who loses their job if circulation declines.

- Being the figurehead for the publication and raising its profile in other media or at business events.

Subbing and editing in the traditional sense can include:

- correcting copy for house style, grammar, spelling;

- checking facts;

- looking for legal issues, e.g. making sure content is not libellous;

- liaising with designers over layout;

- thinking of headlines;

- finding appropriate images;

- being the first port of call for freelancers and taking flak from senior managers.

How to approach editors

There is no single correct way to approach editors, but the process is going to work something like this:

- a brilliant idea comes to you in the middle of the night;

- decide which newspaper or magazine it is suitable for;

- write up your idea into a short concise email outlining the piece;

- wait patiently for reply;

- get commission, agree your rate and set to work.

The truth is that all editors are different. Some will like emails, some will prefer telephone calls. Some editors will be happy to work with you, talk through your idea, give you a steer on what are the most relevant parts and offer helpful suggestions as to whom you might want to speak with.

The important thing to remember is that working relationships take time to foster; getting off on the wrong foot isn't going to help you foster them. Sometimes it is highly tempting to tell editors where to go if they don't accept your ideas, especially if it should happen ten times in a row. From where you sit, an ignored email or phone message brings up all the fear and anxiety you are trying hard to ignore. ('You are rubbish, you will never make it as a writer.' 'Who the hell do you think you are? – go back to the call centre.') This is rubbish – ignore the voices, they exist only in your head! It is time to try again.

It can also be tempting to vent your frustrations on editors, especially if they treat you badly. Yet people have a funny way of cropping up again years later, and people do move from one publication to another. So stay professional and build yourself a good reputation right from the off.

MAKING A PITCH

A good way to think of your pitch is that it is like writing a letter for employment. You need to create a positive professional image by outlining who you are, your relevant experience and the gist of your idea. This will tell your potential client what they can expect in return for relinquishing some of their tight editorial budget.

Pitching by email

Dear Mr Ross,

I am a freelance journalist based in Bristol. I have written for *The Big Issue* and the *Guardian* (for examples, please see my link below).

There is an interesting story happening here which I think would make a great national feature. It is centred around Cycling City (Bristol is the first) and one of its schemes is a pay-by-the-hour 'hire and ride' scheme for bikes that has only previously been seen in Europe.

I suggest a piece talking to the people behind the scheme, plus speaking to some residents of the city to ask them whether they think they will be using the bikes. I'd like to find out if it will be manned in any way. I imagine that if you can pick up bikes in the city centre for £1, they might attract some of the city centre revellers

Many thanks for considering this idea. Please let me know if it is of interest.

Kind regards,

Marc Leverton
Freelance Journalist
Mobile number 12345678
www.website.blogspot.com

Note these aspects of this example pitch email:

■ I have displayed my credentials. I could have attached work if I didn't have a link to a website (which, by the way, is just a free blog site).

■ I have outlined my idea for a feature, why it would be relevant and also suggested an angle.

■ I have used a professional tone while also keeping it lively enough to suggest that I wouldn't bore the pants off their readers if they were to give me the job.

■ The signature also says a lot. Including a surname is more formal than just signing off 'Cheers, Marc', although of course I would do this after I have had a reply and assessed the tone of the conversation.

■ Having a mobile number is also important because it says you can call me anytime. I still use a free email provider because I work from a couple of different computers and want to be able to access my emails wherever I might be.

■ If I was making a written application for something like the work experience I suggest in Chapter 18 'Understanding the media landscape', I would attach some published examples of work I had written plus a CV.

Approaching by phone

Personally, I phone only after I have had a response to an initial email, usually to clarify any points that may have been raised and to make sure that I have a clear understanding of the brief. Phoning at this stage also helps to build the relationship so that if the editor should be unhappy with anything I have produced, they don't mind phoning me back. This helps in getting known as someone who is easy to work with, so that when the option comes around of a commission for another piece, your name is amongst the others in the hat.

If you want to pitch by phone, and there are some editors that respond better to that than others, then it would be well worth finding out what days are good for phoning. Editors are usually very short on time and have to be well organised, having days for writing, commissioning and planning ahead. Again, timing can play a huge part in getting your piece in.

Another approach you may want to take is following up a pitch email with a telephone call. My suggestion is not to be too pushy as it won't take long to get known as 'that pushy freelancer who keeps phoning'. But I also know that follow-up phone calls can work and help to get your pitches noticed by some editors who aren't on top of their emails for whatever reason.

The other benefit of following up with a phone call is that if the editor liked the sound of the idea but didn't reply because it wasn't quite what they were looking for at that time, then your confidence may grow from hearing that you were just a little unlucky that time but that you should keep the ideas coming.

Getting a freelance idea commissioned can take two forms. One is to come up with an idea and pitch and pitch until it finally finds a home. If you really believe in the idea then go for it, but try not to sound desperate or to get angry with editors who don't share your vision. The other approach is just to put that idea on the back burner for now and move on to something else, hopefully to return to it at a later date.

WORKING WITH EDITORS

Beyond approaching editors, you will be working with them and as a freelancer you are always more susceptible to the fickleness of the market, so building a good reputation is essential for the freelancer who wants to continue finding work and getting recommended for more work by word of mouth.

See it from the editor's point of view. They employ a freelance to supply something one of their staff writers can't supply, usually because they are tied to a desk, don't have your contacts or aren't situated where you are.

One of the most common complaints from editors is having to 're-work' pieces that arrive but need more work. As Simon Calder says in the interview in Chapter 7, 'You don't need to be brilliant but you need to be competent, you need to be reliable and know a good story'. Competence and reliability are two skills that some freelancers can forget make working life easier and more stress-free, and this is all that any sensible person should want from their working life.

Tips for building a good reputation

- Be polite, not pushy.

- Be professional by providing the work as agreed, to word count and on deadline. Be early if you can, but not to the detriment of the work.

- Remember at all times that you are working. You must be as professional with the people you are interviewing as you are with the editor.

- Have a portfolio online, which gives details of who you are and what your experience is (such as a mini CV).

- Have a professional signature and a work phone number.

JOURNEY TO PUBLICATION

Stories don't magically appear in magazines and newspapers. The key to being a good freelancer is being proactive, so if the phone doesn't ring, then you need to be the one initiating work for yourself.

The following flow chart should help you to visualise the whole publication process.

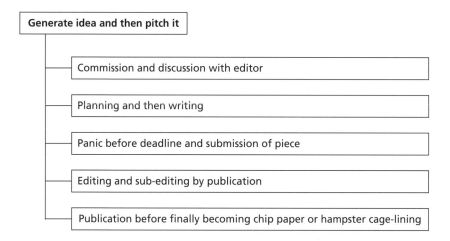

13

The journalist and PR relationship

Definition

Public relations (PR) is the promotion of products, companies and services in the mass media. It is also about managing reputation, be it of an individual or a larger organisation.

PUBLIC RELATIONS, COPYWRITING AND JOURNALISM

Copywriting is the production of words for websites, advertising copy, marketing copy for brochures and press releases. Essentially it is producing words for commerce, which can also be part of the job descriptions for press officers, communications managers and marketing managers.

On some levels, aspects of public relations and copywriting are similar to journalism. Both can involve writing for a defined audience. But the key difference is that PR and copywriting are persuasive writing. The job of the PR or copywriter is to persuade readers to purchase a product or make them aware of the work of a business or organisation. Journalism's role is to inform but also to challenge, discuss, debate, provoke thought and to entertain.

The reason why there is a chapter about PR in this book for freelance journalists is that this is exactly how many journalists make extra revenue. This isn't always an ideal situation, but you need to make a living and the reality is that PR can offer good rewards for your skills. Many talented writers have made a living from PR, advertising and copywriting. If it is good enough for Norman Mailer, Salman Rushdie, William Burroughs, Terry Gilliam, Alan Parker and F. Scott Fitzgerald, then it is good enough for you!

Key points in persuasive writing

■ Identify your target audience.

■ Get on the same level as your audience by speaking the same language.

■ Keep it short and simple.

■ Avoid jargon.

■ Stick to the facts.

Jargon buster

Be aware that 'PR' can mean 'public relations' referring to the industry but it can also mean a press release (you might be told, 'Here is the PR for this'). People working in the industry can also be referred to as a 'PR'. This is highly confusing and a bit silly for the communications industry whose primary function is to communicate messages clearly!

USING PR TO FIND STORIES

Leaving aside the squabbles between journalists and PR that we will look at below, freelancers need stories and the PR industry is knocking out stories every day. It is easier than ever to subscribe to these and signing up for RSS feeds will deliver emails direct from the source.

Be aware that it tends to be the larger organisations which use such technology but local councils and universities, for example, are the kinds of places where a lot of different things are happening all the time. Their emailed newsletters often contain the seeds of some very entertaining stories.

As you make contact with press officers always ask if they can add you to their email lists. A good press officer will tip off journalists that they have a good relationship with, so that journalist can get a head-start on getting a commission before the general press release goes out. So it is worth cultivating these relationships if you think there might be future stories in it.

Once your work is published and your name starts to appear in magazines and newspapers, your details become more and more widely disseminated, and emails from PR companies magically start landing in your email inbox each day. This is a mixed blessing: you have to wade through more and more rubbish, but you never know where and when you are going to find a good source for a story.

HOW TO WRITE A PRESS RELEASE

■ Keep your release to one or two sides of an A4 page.

■ Include a photo if you have one.

■ Bear in mind the date. If you are promoting an event, remember that monthly magazines will want the information a good few weeks before going to press. A daily paper will need just days.

■ Think of what would make a good hook: dates are a natural one.

■ Create some interest if there isn't anything immediate – this is why celebrities open fetes or Page 3 girls open supermarkets.

■ Don't include unnecessary jargon or hyperbole. I have had the dubious pleasure of reading press releases for new products and nobody is going to believe your claims of something being 'revolutionary' or 'fantastic'.

■ Add a few quotes. I have written countless press releases that have simply been recycled into articles in papers – not even recycled sometimes, just cut and pasted. By adding quotes you are doing the journalist's job for them and making it more likely that you will get coverage where and when you want it.

THE JOURNALISM AND PR RELATIONSHIP

Journalism and PR are closely-related industries – both are part of the media machine and both have the same ultimate goal: to get their stories or copy into the media. The difference is that the starting point of 'a story' for a journalist is, well, the story, whereas PR companies are hired by other companies to manage or improve their communications through the media.

PR has a bad reputation with some journalists. There are many reasons for this, some of which are justified and some of which aren't. Essentially what it boils down to is that editorial copy is a more effective advertising medium than paid-for advertising. Readers are, justifiably, more likely to believe a journalist telling them what is the best car to drive than an advertisement for a car. So PR companies cook up as many ideas as possible to try and bag some of this coverage.

Journalists complain of intrusive phone calls. PR people complain that journalists are rude. Journalists say that PR is killing off traditional journalism. PR says that journalists are lazy. They are like a couple of squabbling siblings and it is probably best not to take sides, but just be aware of the arguments of each and maintain your journalistic standards.

The strongest argument against the rise of PR in recent years has come from the journalist Nick Davies who has written a book called *Flat Earth News*. In it he argues that PR companies, press officers in companies and communications managers in local councils have the effect of directing journalists away from finding out any information that may be detrimental to their organisations.

I believe this to be true, and I also believe it is the job of the journalist not to accept stories on face value and to ask questions of everything. There are areas within journalism where this is more true – investigative journalists and news journalists being the obvious examples.

One of the ironies is that despite having said all of the above, many people working in PR trained as journalists and there is a lot of crossover between the two industries in terms of personnel. This is an economic reality as the required skills don't differ greatly. You may hear PR and advertising referred to as 'The Dark Side' by journalists! It is certainly true that they are flip sides of the same coin.

PR writing exercise

Write a press release for an event that you would like to promote. If you can't think of one, have a look on a local listings website, or if you have a Facebook account you will probably know someone who is trying to get you to go to something. Alternatively, you could be aiming to get some publicity for your business or raise some money for charity. Think of the kinds of angles that journalists like to look for and remember the purpose of the press release is to secure media coverage somewhere.

Further reading
- Chartered Institute of Public Relations: www.ipr.org.uk

- www.prweek.com

14

Improving your writing skills

WRITERS ARE MADE, NOT BORN

If you are old enough, you will remember the dance teacher at the beginning of the movie *Fame* who would say, 'Right here is where you start paying, in sweat'.

Writing is a craft, not a god-given gift. Many aspiring writers lack confidence and wish they could write better. The key to writing better is to practise. This is true of so many areas of life. You don't expect to pick up a guitar and play like Jimi Hendrix or kick a football and make David Beckham quake in his boots – the same applies with writing. Everyone starts with some embarrassing teenage rambles but by reading other journalists' work, reading books such as this one and by practising, anyone can become a better writer.

Judge yourself by how you improve. Everyone has a different starting point so measure your progress from where you begin. Don't compare yourself with a top writer, sigh and wistfully think you will never be as good as them. You might not, but they might not have your talent for spotting stories or your access to your local music scene for example.

EXERCISE ROUTINES

So to help you develop your journalistic writing, I suggest working through the exercises for the different styles of journalism included in this book. The exercises begin with writing reviews, as they are short and straightforward. Opinion pieces don't require what journalists call 'legwork' (see Appendix 1, Jargon buster); the better ones tend to rely on tried-and-tested tactics such as shock, outrage, humour and occasionally intelligence.

Remember these are exercises – nobody is assessing them, you can have fun with them and do them as and when you feel suitably inspired. Feel free to make up quotes and be creative if you need to be – remember this is only for practice, to get you used to writing in different styles. Although of course you could use the exercises as a framework for sending pieces in on spec to editors.

THINK BEFORE YOU WRITE

With any piece, think before you write:

- What is it?

- Who will be reading it?

- Should I add quotes?

- Why is this interesting?

- Why would anyone want to read any further?

- What will be my angle?

- Is there anything time relevant?

- Should I point the reader to any further information?

- What section of a publication am I writing for?

MARC'S WRITING AND RE-WRITING TIPS

- Sleep on it or take a break.

- Keep it simple. Go back to your plan.

- Let go. If it doesn't work, say goodbye and move on.

- Don't hold back. Write and then censor or delete it later if needs be!

- Remember that most writing is re-written. Get a rough draft out and then return to the work as many times as is necessary to get it polished up to a standard that you are happy with.

GRAMMAR

I am possibly one of the worst people in the world to be trying to tell anyone else how to improve their grammar. I am constantly being corrected by my students when I write on the whiteboard. The only consolation to be taken from this is if you are thinking that your poor grammar skills might hold you back, they won't. As long as you can write entertaining copy, you will be fine.

There are these fantastically-trained professionals called sub-editors whose job it is to correct poor grammar. It is grammar ignoramuses like me who keep them in work, so I am actually doing the industry a favour.

Further reading

For more writing tips see:

- Marketing guru Matthew Stibbe: http://www.badlanguage. net/27-proven-freelance-marketing-tips

- Food writer Elizabeth Winkler: http://realfoodlover.wordpress. com/winklers-writing-rules/

Improve your grammar by reading:

- *Eats, Shoots & Leaves* by Lynne Truss (Gotham Books) ISBN: 978-1592402038)

15

Media law basics

Media law is a whole subject in itself, and journalism students on NCTJ courses need to pass a Media Law module to gain their qualification. The reason why you need to know something about the law surrounding journalism is so that you don't unwittingly put yourself at risk and find yourself at the wrong end of a court case.

LIBEL LAWS

Libel laws protect individuals, companies, organisations and even products from 'defamation of character'. This is also known as 'slander', which refers to spoken word rather than print.

The tabloids are often involved in these kinds of cases. They print something which is unfounded and false about the private life of a celebrity and they are sued by the likes of Elton John, Madonna or George Michael, or anyone else who can afford good lawyers.

Many journalists have indemnity insurance to protect themselves against being sued for libel. There are specialist companies that can provide this insurance and it is essential for anyone working in news journalism or investigative journalism. The best protection is to write the truth, but with a dark twist of irony this is precisely why some journalists find themselves needing insurance cover.

OFFICIAL SECRETS ACT 1989

The Official Secrets Act is commonly signed by some civil servants and others who work with information pertaining to national security. This basically means that it protects the government from being embarrassed by its employees leaking sensitive material. The signing of the Act is a reminder for employees working with sensitive information; in fact anybody could be prosecuted under the Official Secrets Act, including journalists.

In reality, people do still leak information to the press. When caught they usually claim it is in the 'public interest', which is an expression we are now familiar with. This doesn't mean that, as a journalist, you wouldn't be prosecuted.

FREEDOM OF INFORMATION ACT 2000

This relatively-recent Act has become a great source of stories for journalists who have uncovered spectacular information that would otherwise have remained buried in bureaucracy. Such stories as the various MPs' expense scandals, woeful examples of money wasted by local councils and police officers with criminal records are just a few examples.

The Act introduced a public 'right to know' about any information held by public bodies, including government departments, local councils and schools. A request is made, and the information must be provided within 20 days, as long as finding the information won't cost more than £600. Around 120,000 requests are made each year – 10% of these are made by journalists.

CONTEMPT OF COURT ACT 1981

Journalists covering court cases need to know that it is 'contempt of court' to make an audio recording or take a photograph without the court's consent.

It is not contempt of court (under section 10 of the Act) for a journalist to refuse to disclose their sources, unless the court has considered all the evidence and determined that the information is 'necessary in the interests of justice or national security or for the prevention of disorder or crime'.

COPYRIGHT

Copyright is the legal protection of your intellectual property. Some publications are happy to let you retain copyright; others will want the copyright to your work. And to make things a bit more tricky, you aren't always made aware of which is the case, so the onus is on the journalist to check.

If you did unwittingly hand over your copyright to a publication, and then do what many freelance journalists have done and sell on the piece to another publication, you put yourself in a position where you could be sued for breach of copyright. Yes, even though you are the author of the work.

Further reading
The bible as far as media law is concerned:

- *McNae's Essential Law for Journalists* by David Banks and Mark Hanna (Oxford University Press)
  ISBN: 9780199556458)

16

Media ethics

REPUTATION

Journalists have a pretty poor reputation – some of which is justified but, in my opinion, most of which is not.

This 'image problem' is largely a consequence of the tactics of red-top tabloid journalists, who are a law unto themselves and who operate to a different agenda from the rest of the media. They use techniques that other journalists wouldn't dream of employing, including paying for stories and using aggressive and invasive techniques such as 'door stepping' (see Appendix 1, Jargon buster). This is the equivalent in the written word of the paparazzi, who stalk celebrities or people in the news in order to photograph them as they step out of their houses. These characteristics also make good drama, so on TV and in the movies, journalists tend to be portrayed as the types who would sell their mothers for a story.

Another influence on people's idea of journalists is that they are all like Jeremy Paxman who interrogates politicians on BBC2's *Newsnight* and, quite rightly, has a reputation for not letting them off the hook.

PEOPLE SKILLS

These kinds of journalism have a high profile and subsequently some people might think that they constitute journalism as a whole. If I behaved like Jeremy Paxman when I was interviewing someone for an article in the *Guardian*, it would have the contrary effect to what I needed, and my interviewee would more than likely clam up or run from the room screaming.

Employing the right approach at the right time is down to good people skills. It is people who make stories; like vampires, journalists feed off others. But it is a two-way process, and people also need journalists to spread news, inform the public, create debate, inform and stimulate.

As Mike Jempson says in the interview below, journalists have power. This power needs to be exercised with responsibility and respect.

ASKING QUESTIONS

Employing people skills doesn't mean allowing things to go unquestioned – part of the journalist's job is to ask the questions that others aren't asking. This performs an important role for democracy, but it is also going to get you good copy, which in turn will lead to more work. So there is actually a selfish element to asking good questions.

The truth is that a very high percentage of journalism jobs are a lot less invasive than the media stereotypes. Sometimes a journalist might face a dilemma when writing about a sensitive issue and editors are often as uncertain as journalists as to how some stories should be covered. So if you are ever unsure, ask your editor for guidance first, but if they are uncertain or too busy to deal with the issue, there are guidelines for many sensitive subjects such as suicide or immigration on the MediaWise website (www.mediawise.org.uk).

'OFF THE RECORD'

Another dilemma might arise if a contact you are speaking to asks for something to be 'off the record', meaning that they will give you the information but the information must not be attributed to them. This commonly arises when you are researching background information for a story. Journalists often get around it by saying things like, 'A source close to Cabinet said…' or 'The rumour amongst Whitehall is that…'.

'Off the record' should be respected for the sake of other journalists. Journalists aren't trusted at the best of times and behaving in an ethical manner will boost your own personal reputation and the reputation of journalists collectively. Also, if you develop trust with your sources, they may come back to you in the future with further potential stories.

POLITICAL CORRECTNESS

One of the areas in which journalists can blunder into trouble is in their choice of words. Some people suggest that political correctness is a form of censorship. Perhaps the best advice here is to think of the audience first and work out what would be acceptable to them. Obviously the *Daily Mail* has a different take on this from the *Guardian*. Some of these issues are tackled in the style guides written by newspapers for their contributors.

PRESS COMPLAINTS COMMISSION – CODE OF PRACTICE

The Press Complaints Commission (PCC) deals with complaints made by the public regarding the press. Such complaints may include information printed in an article, the way someone or something has been portrayed, or a journalist's individual behaviour.

Outside legal issues (see Chapter 15, Media Law), the newspaper and magazine publishing industry is self-regulated. The PCC has devised a Code of Practice that serves as an excellent guideline. The Code can be read or downloaded as a PDF (at www.pcc.org. uk/cop/practice.html); below are some of the key sections.

---

1 Accuracy

i)   The Press must take care not to publish inaccurate, misleading or distorted information, including pictures.

ii) A significant inaccuracy, misleading statement or distortion once recognised must be corrected, promptly and with due prominence, and – where appropriate – an apology published.

iii) The Press, whilst free to be partisan, must distinguish clearly between comment, conjecture and fact.

iv) A publication must report fairly and accurately the outcome of an action for defamation to which it has been a party, unless an agreed settlement states otherwise, or an agreed statement is published.

2 Opportunity to reply

A fair opportunity for reply to inaccuracies must be given when reasonably called for.

---

3 *Privacy

i)   Everyone is entitled to respect for his or her private and family life, home, health and correspondence, including digital communications.

ii) Editors will be expected to justify intrusions into any individual's private life without consent. Account will be taken of the complainant's own public disclosures of information.

iii) It is unacceptable to photograph individuals in private places without their consent.

Note – Private places are public or private property where there is a reasonable expectation of privacy.

4 Harassment

i)   Journalists must not engage in intimidation, harassment or persistent pursuit.

ii) They must not persist in questioning, telephoning, pursuing or photographing individuals once asked to desist; nor remain on their property when asked to leave and must not follow them. If requested, they must identify themselves and whom they represent.

iii) Editors must ensure these principles are observed by those working for them and take care not to use non-compliant material from other sources.

...

12 Discrimination

i)   The press must avoid prejudicial or pejorative reference to an individual's race, colour, religion, gender, sexual orientation or to any physical or mental illness or disability.

ii) Details of an individual's race, colour, religion, sexual orientation, physical or mental illness or disability must be avoided unless genuinely relevant to the story.

13 Confidential sources

Journalists have a moral obligation to protect confidential sources of information.

> **14 Witness payments in criminal trials**
> No payment or offer of payment to a witness – or any person
> who may reasonably be expected to be called as a witness –
> should be made in any case once proceedings are active as
> defined by the Contempt of Court Act 1981.
>
> This prohibition lasts until the suspect has been freed
> unconditionally by police without charge or bail or the
> proceedings are otherwise discontinued; or has entered a guilty
> plea to the court; or, in the event of a not guilty plea, the court
> has announced its verdict.
>
> ...

Further reading

- *Flat Earth News* by Nick Davies (Chatto & Windus)

- *Can You Trust the Media?* by Adrian Monck with Mike Hanley
  (Icon Books)

- *The Ethical Journalist* by Tony Harcup (Sage)

- *Ethics for Journalists* by Richard Keeble (Routledge)

Interview: **Mike Jempson, MediaWise**

> Mike Jempson is the director of MediaWise (originally PressWise),
> a charity set up to research and support victims of media abuse.
>
> www.mediawise.org.uk

What is the role of MediaWise?
MediaWise was set up in 1993 by victims of the media, people
whose lives had been wrecked by bad journalism. There had
been numerous attempts to look at reform systems through

statutory changes through the 'right to reply' and the creation of an independent body which could examine people's complaints. When these attempts didn't work, these people came together and they suggested that three things should be provided:

- There should be someone who can immediately spring into action and tell people what to do. They said they found their situation a very frightening experience and also very isolating.
- They said that they needed to speak to someone who knew what they were going through.
- And that a system should operate so that others didn't have to go through what they had.

We interpreted this last point to develop training and guidelines so journalists could do their jobs better.

So we listen very carefully and we examine the stories that people have been a part of. We advise on what they can do for redress or explain that they don't have a case.

When you say 'bad journalism', what exactly do you mean?
It often involves very silly mistakes, which may have crept into the process rather than being something deliberately done by an individual. Sometimes it is a journalist being overly intrusive, or they may have applied methods that aren't acceptable or may even be illegal.

Silly little mistakes can have enormous consequences and this is often the result of poor subbing or thoughtlessness. For example, a local newspaper could publish a story of someone in a street dying and mention that the whole street will be going to the funeral at such and such a time. That is just not very bright subbing, someone should have noticed.

Other times people are tricked or threatened into saying something they don't want to say. A bad example of this was a journalist walking around the outside of a house hounding a woman who was a teacher and who had once worked as an escort saying, 'Come out, we know you are in there. Come out and tell us about your life as a prostitute'. That is completely unacceptable behaviour.

Sometimes it is just an interpretation put on a story and it is difficult to make a complaint about it because it is only implied. It doesn't end up in black and white and wouldn't be supported by the Press Complaints Commission. The only codes we have in journalism are those laid down by the PCC.

How can journalists themselves ensure their work is ethical?
First of all, you have to feel comfortable that what you do is justifiable in terms of what you are setting out to achieve. You might want to climb the career ladder quickly and will do anything for your editor, or you may be a freelancer hoping to get work. You have to examine your own conscience and see what is justifiable to you to get the story. If a journalist has to do something in the public interest, do the means suit the ends? You can't just say, 'Well, the editor told me to do it.'

We have to impress on the powers that be that we want to behave ethically and it isn't just about money.

Do journalists ever contact MediaWise with queries?
Yes, including some very well known names. A newsreader who wasn't happy with the scripting called us recently. Often, on the job, people are under considerable pressure and don't get a chance to talk about these issues. I think journalists should talk to each other about some of these things. I am quite proud of the fact that TV researchers and producers have all called us saying they aren't sure about something and what do we think.

The NUJ [National Union of Journalists] also has an ethics helpline, which will put journalists in touch with someone who can help them.

There is a thin line between 'doing the job' of asking questions and overstepping the mark. I don't think journalists know what power they have. If someone experiences an inaccuracy in the press, in their minds they think that all the public will have noticed. I know a woman who didn't leave the house for 12 years after the way she was treated by a journalist. Her children were targeted, and the children's friends were offered money to talk and she was understandably terrified by this behaviour. I think this is a case when journalists should have been asking themselves questions.

Journalists should never be afraid to ask a question, but they also need to know that not everyone is obliged to answer that question. Someone might have a very good reason for not answering and that doesn't mean they are guilty. If I say 'No' twice, then that should be enough.

Are the tabloids more at fault than the rest of the press?
You can't use a broad brush – a lot can be in local papers. There is a tendency to look for 'victims' in the tabloids and celebrities are getting tougher with their privacy, so the chances of a member of the public coming a cropper are increasing.

There is also the *Daily Mail* – we have had a lot of complaints about the way that they construct their stories. But we have also had complaints about all the other papers as well: *The Times*, the *Telegraph*, the *Guardian*. It happens right across the board and many complaints are about magazines like *Chat* and the life story magazines.

Does bringing money into the scenario confuse things?
The problem is that the public is very keen to help. The contracts I have seen written by newspapers aren't worth the paper that they are written on, and they always ask for maximum information. What they are buying is people's silence. I often use the example where the publication offers a great deal of money for a splash and spread. And then they run something much smaller and offer a couple of hundred quid instead of the several thousand that they promised.

What else would make the media more responsible?
One approach could be taking an ethical stance, measured in a corporate social responsibility [CSR] report. This would ensure media organisations take responsibility for the quality of their journalism. Having journalists scared for their jobs isn't going to develop this kind of culture. I would prefer there to be some CSR which looks at the number of complaints made, the number of

corrections, mistakes and errors, and perhaps some stuff about media training.

Do you have any specific advice for freelance journalists?
One of the most important things is never to offer what you can't produce. One of the biggest changes in my career was that you would have made a pitch saying, 'I want to find out if there is a story here', but now you have to say, 'I know there is a story here'.

There is a tendency to over-egg the pudding: people pitch before they know. And if you have it all sewn up it is easy for people to nick the story. So it is a difficult situation.

Some people think it doesn't matter, but it does matter – I know people who have killed themselves because of what journalists have written. Journalists should want to be popular, not with the rich and powerful or the politicians. We should reject this notion that we are down there with estate agents in terms of popularity. People should want us and not fear us.

Part Two

The business of freelancing

17

Stepping into the unknown

THE 'AM I UP TO IT?' SKILLS TEST

The words 'skills test' probably sound incredibly frightening and as soon as you read them you may have automatically assumed you wouldn't match up. Don't stop reading here – you are about to discover a secret about the working world.

First, let us consider a few skills that are needed by a journalist:

■ an understanding of different writing styles;

■ interviewing techniques;

■ ability to meet deadlines.

And some additional attributes which might be useful:

■ curiosity;

■ shorthand;

■ a good way with people;

■ an eye for a story.

There are some further things we can add for working freelance:

■ organisational skills;

■ time management skills;

■ tenacity;

■ a thick skin;

■ financial management skills.

These lists aren't exhaustive; you may want to add some of your own ideas.

When I go through this process in my classes, I ask the whole class to shout out their ideas for journalism skills and freelance skills. We usually manage to fill a whole whiteboard – it is enough to put anyone off ever attempting either! Do you have all these skills and attributes? No, I know you don't. How do I know? Because nobody does! If you do, what are you doing reading this book? You should be a millionaire already and be sunning yourself on your own private beach.

Seriously though, I can honestly say that most journalists I know probably have half of these skills. You could take the same exercise and apply it to any job. In reality, anybody in any job finds that some of the required skills come naturally, and they need to work at the others. When I was a manager, I was required to do monthly appraisals with staff, and had them myself. On so many of those occasions, staff would have their reasons to be praised and the same 'must develop' points each month. Nobody is perfect – get over it and get on with it.

I can say that I do not possess all the journalistic and freelance skills I have outlined above and yet I have managed to make a living and even get this book published. I think it is realistic to suggest that you already have 50% of these skills, and the other 50% you can work at. Some of those weak points may even turn out to be strengths eventually.

WRITING ABILITY

When I first made the leap from part-time journalism to full-time, I met with an old editor friend of mine. I expressed my fear that I didn't know if I was a good enough writer. He nodded and said, 'Don't worry, it will come'. And he was right. After getting away with a few articles which, looking back, were adequate but weren't really Pulitzer Prize contenders, I felt that I was gaining confidence and pushing myself to try out some of the new writing techniques that I was learning.

I was reading pieces by journalists every day, but not reading them for the content. I was looking at how they were structured, what the journalist had chosen to include and taking an educated guess at what they might not have put in. I also thought about how they might have pitched the articles and what angle they had chosen to take.

After a little while, I began to feel that I understood the media in a whole new way. Everything you read in a paper or online or see on TV has been constructed by someone else. There are certain guidelines to be followed but these can be learnt and don't come from any divine source.

This brings me back to a point I made earlier and one of my motivations for writing this book: new journalists need guidance through the media jungle. Journalists generally are in fear of losing their jobs at the moment and many staff writers are being laid off from evening newspapers, creating ever more freelancers chasing the same number of opportunities. So from sheer competition you need to assess your skills and work at the weaker sides of your game. Short courses and further training opportunities are listed in Appendix 3 'Further Training'.

Any job skill for any profession can be developed and improved. There are also many levels within the journalism profession. Writing for local newspapers and niche publications is a different ball game from writing for national titles. Work out which kinds of publications suit you, what your interests are and what further training you need.

FINDING ENCOURAGEMENT FROM A MENTOR

You might encounter some people who might not be particularly encouraging or helpful. Differentiating between helpful advice and negativity is tricky. If you can, find someone who believes in your ability and arrange to meet them every now and then to talk about your progress.

If you can formalise this arrangement so that they become your mentor, this would be even better. It is better still if your mentor is also a journalist, but the important thing is that there is some support for you as you undertake this new challenge.

We all have doubting voices in our heads and having someone believe in us can make all the difference. I believe in you. I have seen all kinds of people become journalists, some with very poor social skills. If they can do it, I have no doubt that you can.

PROFESSIONAL JEALOUSY

If you do know some journalists already, you might not feel encouraged by them at this moment because the industry is going through some turmoil and there is a lot of competition for work. My advice is to ignore such discouragement and go and find out for yourself. The only person who can find out what you are capable of is you.

Professional jealousy is rife and it took me a long time to work out what it was. Other journalists may fear you stealing their ideas or their clients. They might even begrudge your success – 'I have been published by *The Times*!' might be met with 'Those bastards never respond to my emails' rather than 'Well done, you'. But this is just professional jealousy and you must take it as a compliment.

In reality, the more aspiring journalists I meet, the more I am amazed at the sheer breadth of different niches that people aspire to write about: anti-airport expansion, horses and gas pipes are three real-life examples I have encountered.

Stepping into the unknown will take you on a journey. Journalism is more a career than a job, and it is difficult to clock in and out. After a while you notice that you are looking for stories 24/7. I have interviewed my father-in-law, and met an editor and exchanged business cards at my daughter's ballet class. I really don't switch that part of me off – I know that may be sad to some people, but I think you have got to take opportunities wherever you find them.

Gaining industry experience

Okay, so you have tried the writing exercises in Part One (or already have some experience) and have decided that you want to push on to the next level. Good for you. Now it is time to research some new places for you to work. As with any job, the more you know about how an industry operates the better.

THE MEDIA LANDSCAPE

'The media' is a generic term for TV, radio, internet and traditional printed newspapers and magazines. People who say they are working in 'the media' could mean anything from being a film director to selling classified advertising on a local free ads paper.

'New media' refers to anything that is published online and can include producing content through editorial, podcasts or social networking/marketing.

For most new journalists hoping to get their words published, online and local opportunities provide the easiest routes. There are many websites now dedicated to reviews that rely on content from part-time writers. Online provides so many opportunities because the overheads are a lot less than setting up traditional print media with its expensive print and distribution costs. Almost every business has a website these days. Strictly speaking, writing for a website is copywriting rather than journalism, but it can provide an opportunity to put something in your portfolio and to get more familiar with writing for a specific audience.

CHECK YOUR LOCAL MEDIA: WHAT IS OUT THERE?

Evening papers

Evening papers are the most prominent outlet for journalists locally and many do offer some freelance opportunities even if they don't tend to be among the better paid. The last few years have seen a huge downturn in the numbers of staff writers employed, resulting from declining numbers of readers and declining advertising revenues. So the picture is pretty gloomy but don't let that put you off. Even if you get only one piece published and you don't get paid much for it, it will look good in your portfolio and may lead you to bigger and brighter things.

The trick to getting published in your local paper is fostering contact with the commissioning editor. They may be snowed under with piles of work and requests from freelancers, but you must try anyway.

Listings magazines

Time Out-style magazines usually have some kind of presence in cities of a decent size. These are ideal for younger writers who like to write about local bands and theatre, or to review clubs and places for eating out. Again, budgets can be tight but seeing bands for free or getting a free CD or meal can make up for the lack of silver crossing your palm.

Student magazines

Student magazines are of course great if you are a student. The Guardian Media Student Awards highlight the best of each year's crop, and an award is excellent for future career prospects and your CV.

I used to write for *S-Press* while at Sheffield Hallam University and I also wrote and read the news for Forge FM, which was a community radio station. These stayed on my CV for years and years, and I know this experience counted for a lot in getting my job at *The Big Issue*. These voluntary positions also taught me many of the basic journalism skills that I needed and built upon in later years. In addition you never know when you will meet colleagues again and it isn't unheard of for people to make acquaintances who open doors again much later.

District freebies

These publications are often advertising-led and varied in quality but don't rule them out – my local freebie in Bristol, *Bishopston Matters*, has many interesting features and provides a valuable community resource. These types of publications are often run on a very tight budget with only one or two people involved, but they can provide an opportunity to write about something particularly relevant in your neighbourhood. This is great if you have a specialism in say local history, or are hoping to publicise an event at your local school.

Review websites

If you want to get used to having your reviews seen by other people, websites like The Book Bag and Amazon provide an opportunity to write short reviews and for readers to indicate whether they found them useful or not.

Radio stations

One of my first journalism jobs was writing and reading the news on a community radio station. This experience taught me a lot about how to construct the news and where news stories were found. See the information on gaining experience on local radio stations in the following section on 'Volunteering'.

SHOULD I WORK FOR FREE?

Nobody can afford to work for free forever. My advice is that you use it to get the relevant experience that you need to find you the paid job you want, whether that is part-time, full-time or freelance.

Be aware, however, that there are serious concerns within journalism that work experience people, interns and volunteers can be exploited. Some unscrupulous organisations simply replace one work experience person with another, with no intention of ever offering a paid position.

My advice is that before you start, you agree exactly what you will be doing and the terms and conditions of the placement. Make sure that you go into the organisation knowing what to expect so you aren't later disappointed that all you got to do was make tea.

GETTING THE BALANCE RIGHT

I started out working for free, doing short music reviews wherever I could. I gained from this as I built up industry experience, but you do have to draw the line at some stage. I suggest that the difference between being an amateur and a professional, as with a sports person, is getting paid for it. You can't afford to be an amateur forever and you need to prepared to say 'No' (with a capital N) if someone is blatantly trying to pull a fast one. You owe it to yourself and all those who follow behind you.

Sometimes it is the bigger companies and organisations that are the worst culprits. In these cases you need to weigh up how much clout that organisation's name is going to have on your CV.

Also, preferably before you leave, make sure you get the all-important reference or testimonial that can be used in the future. These days references just confirm that you did indeed do work experience when you say you did, without referring to your unique qualities. A personal testimonial might say, 'Liz writes beautifully and always hit her deadlines. I don't hesitate in recommending her.' Signed: 'Jesus H, Editor of *Blasphemy Monthly*.' You often see freelance journalists putting these kinds of statements on their websites.

INTERNSHIPS

An 'internship' is a nice term imported from the US, which is a glorified version of what we always called 'work experience' in the UK. The deal is that you can work for much longer, say six months or a year, and receive only the minimum wage.

This point is very important as, under the National Minimum Wage Act 1998, if someone is a 'worker' (i.e. they are under a contract), then they must be paid at least the minimum wage, regardless of their job title. Young people still at school do not qualify for the minimum wage and neither do students doing work experience as part of their studies, provided the placement is less than a year. Also if the work experience is just 'shadowing' a worker, they will not qualify for the minimum wage.

VOLUNTEERING

Volunteering is a different prospect and volunteers can work for charities for free, gaining work experience and doing something for others at the same time. This is a great way to gain some relevant experience. There is the occasional magazine or newspaper put together by volunteers but it certainly won't harm your cause to look for opportunities in similar organisations that utilise many of the same skills required by journalism.

One of the benefits of finding a project run by volunteers is that there is often a Volunteer Manager who is used to working with volunteers. You won't be the lone 'work experience person' that nobody quite knows what to do with. They are more likely to have a training programme and be understanding if you were to land yourself a job.

Volunteering in communications for a local charity

Local charities often need help with their communications work as this is an area that many can't afford to employ someone for.

Look through your local paper – I guarantee there is a charity-related story in almost every edition: 'Man cycles for 24 hours in aid of dog home', 'Student sits in beans for a week to raise vital funds for Beanaholics Anonymous', 'Octogenarian Brenda parachutes for Africa'.

This kind of PR work, generating stories on a charity's behalf, will help you to develop contacts and also make you aware of the types of stories that catch editors' attention. It also provides an enormous sense of satisfaction, as charities can attract further funding or donations through media attention, meaning your work will be well appreciated.

COMMUNITY RADIO

Broadcast media is a kind of sister to traditional print journalism. Many people working in radio have also worked on newspapers and are known as 'broadcast journalists'. On a local level there are more community radio stations than ever before: 162 in the UK at the time of writing, and if you volunteer you would be amazed at the amount of knowledge you can pick up. There doesn't seem to be a great deal of money to be made in radio, which is a shame for the aspiring professional, but that doesn't mean you shouldn't do it if it is an ambition of yours. You might just have to hang onto that other job a little bit longer and volunteer to do the graveyard shift at the local radio station.

The Community Media Association includes details of community radio stations around the country on their website: www. commedia.org.uk

HOSPITAL AND STUDENT RADIO

Hospital and student radio can be an excellent way to learn about the medium and get a foot on the career ladder – it's where almost a third of Radio 1 presenters got their start. Radio 1's Huw Stephens remembers how his career began: 'In school I managed a friend's band and loved listening to the radio at night. I got to help out at my local hospital radio station in Cardiff, sorting out the records and putting them back tidily on the shelves. After a while doing that and sitting in on other shows and practising a lot, I got to present my own show once a week. The experience was so enjoyable, and a perfect start to a career in radio.'

There are 228 hospital radio stations in the UK, with almost 2,000 volunteers aiming to make patients' stays a little better. The BBC often call hospital radio their training ground and will suggest to aspiring DJs to get experience there first.

COMMUNITY SERVICE VOLUNTEER ACTION DESKS

Community Service Volunteer (CSV) has a unique relationship with the BBC, providing 200 volunteers to 36 different BBC local radio stations across the country through their network of Action Desks. The CSV Action Desks are run by a CSV producer who works with BBC colleagues to produce great content for radio, TV and online.

Damian Radcliffe runs the Action Desk programme for CSV. Having worked for community and commercial radio stations himself, he knows what it takes to make a career in broadcasting. 'Nothing works better than knowing your stuff and being passionate about radio – you really need to do your homework. We have a huge demand for voluntary places and we are often more interested in attitude than aptitude. You can teach the skills but not that intrinsic interest in the world about you.'

Opportunities with CSV reflect the diversity of positions in radio stations. 'It isn't just about being the next Chris Moyles,' Damian says. 'You may specialise or you may be a bit of a jack of all trades. There are many other elements to radio such as production, editing, sales and marketing.'

Many CSV volunteers have gone on to work in radio, including James King the Radio 1 film critic.

LOOKING FOR WORK EXPERIENCE OPPORTUNITIES

Try local newspapers and magazines, using the information provided above as a guide to where you think will suit you best. Approach them with a formal letter, CV and an example of your writing.

Some opportunities crop up on the jobs listings sites:

- www.journalism.co.uk

- www.pressgazette.co.uk

You can also look in the media section of Guardian Jobs:

- www.jobs.guardian.co.uk

Further information

- www.csv.org.uk

- www.hbauk.co.uk

- www.commedia.org.uk

- www.volunteering.org.uk/IWantToVolunteer

19

Marketing yourself

BUILDING A PORTFOLIO

One of the key things to remember in this whole process is that you are trying to convince an editor, who has never met you or seen your work before, to part with a portion of their ever-tightening budget. So why the hell should they give it to you?

- Because your idea is good. Okay.

- Because you sound like you know what you are talking about. Okay.

- Because you have also suggested that you may have some other good ideas after this one. Well done.

But what the editor really wants to know above everything else is whether or not you can deliver what you say you are going to: 'Will I have to spend ages editing this person's work, getting it fit for publication, or will it just slot straight into the paper without me having to do a complete re-write?'

A portfolio does all of the above. It is a massive self-advertisement that says, 'Look at me, aren't I great? I have written for all these different people on all these different topics.' I think an online portfolio looks the most professional because it suggests that you have had so much work published that you can fill a whole website. It also shows that you are capable of dealing with blogging tools.

Everyone has to start with getting a few bits and pieces published wherever they can. If it is in print media, see if you can get hold of the PDFs of the published pages that include your work. The final printed version looks far more professional than a Word document, accompanied by just your word that it was actually printed in the *Glasgow Herald*.

This is also another reason why the byline is so important. Journalists love seeing their names in print of course but there are professional reasons why people need to know who the authors of pieces are. Plus it allows the reader to keep an eye on their favourite writers, and the wronged celeb to know exactly who to sue.

ONLINE FREELANCE DIRECTORIES

There are lots of freelance directories online, suggesting that editors might trawl through them and then contact you to offer you lots of money to work for them. They won't. I have registered with many of these directories and have had just one email from a trade magazine that was good to work for, but whose accounts department was based in Eastern Europe and took the best part of three months from my invoice date to pay.

The one good thing these online directories do is to back up that you are who you say you are. I often suggest to editors that they can look on my website to see some examples of my work, or they can Google 'Marc Leverton', as this brings up work I have had published by the *Guardian* as well as several of the sites which list me as a freelance journalist – always handy when you are trying to persuade someone to invest some money in you.

NETWORKING GROUPS

Most cities have groups that can help you to get out there and create some contacts. Nothing happens in isolation – journalists mostly report on what other people are up to. In Bristol, where I live, there is a media group that meets once a month, the local branch of the NUJ organises occasional meetings for freelance journalists to exchange ideas, and there are also networking events arranged by an organisation that promotes small businesses.

It is also true that people tend to commission people who they like. So if you make the effort to get on with people and become known as someone who is good at their job and good to work with, then this in itself will lead to more work.

WORD OF MOUTH

Building relationships is the key to finding people who you can continue to work with. It is fine to write a piece for someone and then move on to another magazine, but this isn't going to lead to a successful well-paid career. To do that, you need to have several clients who are regulars whom you can approach and know that they are going to at least say, 'Sorry, not this time but keep the ideas coming'.

For more tips on working and building relationships with editors, refer to Chapter 12 'How to approach editors'.

AM I SELLING OUT?

Freelancing is about being proactive and creating opportunities that bring you work: pitching ideas, networking and letting people know that you are freelance and available for work. This is a big part of freelancing; you can't assume that you will be spending 37 hours a week writing articles.

Many journalists are uncomfortable with the idea of 'selling themselves'. There may be several reasons for this: it could be perceived as demeaning or an admission that you are somehow not good enough to attract regular work. Remember, a freelancer is only going to get paid for what they produce, so get out there and build up a thick skin.

GET OUT THERE

I often describe the process of selling myself as 'tarting about', or 'trying to flog my wares'. This might take some of the shine off the glamour of working as a journalist, but it's the reality of a tough old job.

To quote a couple of other well-worn clichés, a lot of the skill in freelancing is being in the right place at the right time, and work tends to lead to more work. So get out there, email everyone you know to tell them you are looking for work and start by pitching some ideas. Staying at home and waiting for the phone to ring isn't going to bring you the levels of work that you require to pay your bills. If you have contacts, use them. If you don't have contacts, create them.

ONLINE SOCIAL NETWORKING

Social networking is largely a means for marketing yourself, and includes Twitter, Facebook and LinkedIn. I am also including blogging with this section, even though it involves a bit more than just networking. Some people might argue that blogging would be better included in Part 1 of this book along with the other styles of journalistic writing. But in my opinion social networking is not a replacement for journalism and should only add to your work as a journalist and provide you with more ammunition to do your job.

In the olden days freelancers relied on networking techniques such as taking people out to lunch, going for a coffee, popping into the office to say hello. Social networking is basically doing the same thing, but online rather than in the 'real world'.

Networking has always been about relationship building and reminding people that you exist and are available for work.

The benefit of online social networking is that it works exactly as above, but you don't need to leave the house (which is great if you live a distance from your client). Popularised by teenagers, the sites have passed into the realm of 'oldies' who generally have more to sell and save than teenagers who, understandably, want to chat and play games.

The flip side of the coin is that you can spend more time networking than actually working. I don't want to spoil your fun, but a successful freelancer is a working freelancer so this is an important balance to get right.

SHOULD I HAVE A BLOG?

It seems everyone has a blog these days and they are very simple to create – the trick is attracting readers to it. There are some familiar things to think about before diving in. Who is going to read your blog? What angle are you going to take? Random posts about things that you find funny can be good for your friends, but will they really appeal to an audience beyond them?

Another important consideration is that blogging isn't necessarily a means to an end financially. There are many bloggers out there who can make some money from advertising but they are the minority rather than the norm.

One thing that blogging can do is to keep you on the radar of commissioning editors. There are increasing opportunities for bloggers to link into newspaper websites. The *Guardian*, for example, includes a blog with almost every section now, providing online content of which only a small percentage makes its way into the printed paper. Also, the *Guardian*'s 'Comment Is Free' section picks out contributions from the best political and comment sites and even reports directly from politicians' own blogs.

There is another form of blogging which is tagged a 'brag'. If you are lucky enough to have hit a seam of freelancing that takes you to unusual places to meet unusual people you might want to brag about this, link to your work and demonstrate your ability to write in a variety of styles.

Essentially blogging is a good calling card; it might open some doors for you if you are lucky and focused. It requires a lot of regular updating and needs to be as focused on its subject as any other piece of writing. It is very easy to fall into the ramblings of a mentalist territory.

BLOGGING AND JOURNALISM

There aren't that many examples out there of people who make a transition from blogging to journalism, but this case is a glorious exception. Matt Drudge was a loner working in a gift shop in LA in the 1990s. He ran a blog on the comings and goings of celebs in Hollywood … well, he did until he came across a big story. That story was the details of Monica Lewinsky's affair with Bill Clinton which eventually led to his impeachment. Possibly one of the biggest stories of the entire decade. Drudge was subsequently offered a 'proper journalism job' at AOL.

BLOG AS PORTFOLIO

I have a blog, which isn't full of my ramblings about my life but rather is a place for me to upload articles that I have had published. My email signature includes a link to this website and it receives a steady stream of nosey people who want to check out my work. It saves me having to attach bits of work to prove to editors that I can do the job.

I once paid a freelance designer to make a website for me. She did a great job, but every time I wanted to add something I had to contact her and pay for her time. Eventually she emigrated and went completely incommunicado, leaving me with a static website that I could do nothing with until eventually the domain name expired.

You can avoid this situation by choosing a website design that will allow you to make your own updates, using a content management system. If you do choose to let a designer build the site for you, at the time of commissioning check the process for updating the site, whether there will be any further costs for updates and how much control you will have in the future.

TWITTER

Twitter tells people about whatever you choose to tell them, up to a maximum of 140 characters. This doesn't sound like much, but Twitter came to prominence when Steven Fry started a celebrity trend of telling his fans whatever he was up to – including getting stuck in a lift. It gained more serious notoriety during riots in Iran. The US refused to close the site down and protesters were able to tell the outside world what was happening.

Back in the rest of the world, you can use Twitter to look for stories by signing up to 'sources' such as PR people and people who operate within your own niche and journalistic interests.

I hate Twitter because I don't want to tell people every time I make a cup of tea or go for a pee. Having said that, I have seen it used to great effect by people who are trying to promote something. The better you are known, the better it seems to work. Charlie Brooker had readers send him words to inspire a column and Steven Fry seems to spend his life 'tweeting'. If it keeps you in the minds of commissioning editors that is good. If it provides you with story leads then that is also great.

FACEBOOK

Using Facebook as a social networking tool shouldn't need an introduction here, but stories can also be found through it. Gigs are promoted, for example, and groups reflect niche interests. The important thing to remember for any kind of journalism is that before anything can be written about, someone needs to get up and make something happen. Facebook is the perfect place for people to shout about the fact that they are arranging something worthy of you writing about it.

Facebook is also slightly different in that you can use it for real networking. I have found subjects to interview by putting requests out on Facebook and have also approached contacts that I may have otherwise been unable to contact. In fact the Damian Barr interview on page 74 is an example of this.

LINKEDIN

LinkedIn works along similar lines to Facebook but is primarily there to foster business networking. I use it and have uploaded details about myself and an outline of my CV. I am 'linked in' with many publishing industry professionals, although it doesn't seem to have led directly to any work as yet. Much like the journalism directories sites mentioned above, it doesn't cost anything and it only takes securing one job for it to have been worthwhile.

The important thing to remember with all social networking is that it is a tool to help you get more stories or promote your career in some way. Don't get distracted from that objective and spend your valuable time looking at pictures of your mates. Remember when you are freelance, your time is your own.

Interview: **Matthew Stibbe, Articulate Marketing**

Matthew Stibbe is writer in chief at Articulate Marketing (www. articulatemarketing.com). Previously, he was a freelance journalist writing about aviation, business and technology for *Wired* and business magazines. His writing blog – www.BadLanguage.Net – receives 1,500 visitors a month and his '27 tips for freelance journalists' is one of his highest-read posts.

Are journalists very good at marketing themselves?
I have met quite a few freelance writers who tend to feel a bit backward about coming forward, but this is common amongst small business people. The reality is that you have to do more than just set up before the phone starts to ring.

There are so many ways of finding journalists now, and there is all this competition out there. Someone said to me that freelance journalists are the battered wives of the media! They get their work butchered and are paid very badly.

Marketing is partly about increasing your workload but it is also about increasing your reputation so that you can charge more for your services.

So how should journalists market themselves?
The number one tip I have is 'the daily pitch'. If you do this first thing in the morning, it is just a small daily habit. If there are 240 working days a year then that is 240 pitches. And eventually once you get known, editors will start asking you for stuff.

What shouldn't a freelance journalist do in the search for work?
Working relationships are easy to destroy by being late for a meeting or missing a deadline, for example. It should go without saying, but just doing a bad job – all the work should be factually

correct and double-checked. Then there is simply bad writing, where people are padding out for the word count.

I worked for a while as a sub-editor and the amount of re-writing I used to have to do was shocking. What an editor wants is something bang on time, nicely written and if I phone someone featured in an interview they say, 'Yes, I said that'. Subbing was a grisly experience and a real eye opener. For practice, you can sub-edit work that is already published; you will be amazed at how many mistakes make it into the press every day.

Are blogs a good form of marketing?
They can secure your reputation but I don't know if they will bring you much freelance work. What is useful about them is that they give you a place to practise writing. Having said that you certainly need a website to show examples of your work and things like Facebook, XING, LinkedIn and Twitter are all good ways to link in with editors.

Do you still work as a freelance journalist?
I have become a corporate writer after spending some time as a freelance journalist. I work for Hewlett Packard, Microsoft, eBay and parts of the government. It is essentially the same work but you get treated better and paid more in the corporate market.

But it is still absolutely possible to make a living from being a journalist. I think the freelance way is possibly harder and tougher than working as a staff writer but it's still achievable if you find a good niche.

How did you make this move into corporate writing?
I was writing for a magazine about research and development for Microsoft. About a week later I got a call from Microsoft asking me if I would like to write a small booklet for them. So within a short period of time I had moved into corporate work. I was paid better and treated better so it was quite easy to turn my back on journalism, although I think of what I do now as being a corporate journalist.

Do you have any other tips for aspiring journalists and writers?
I suggest keeping a notebook of ideas – you never know when inspiration will strike. I also found it useful to make lists of the magazines that I wanted to work for. I was desperate to work for *Wired* as I loved the magazine so much.

The most powerful sentence in the world is 'Can you help me?' It is much more likely that you will elicit a response from this than just wading straight in with a pitched idea.

If you are completely new I'd also suggest getting a mentor. I used to review gadgets and I was helped so much by the editor of the magazine that I was working for.

20

Planning, organisation and time management

COMMON FREELANCE PITFALLS AND SOLUTIONS

Being aware of some of the pitfalls that other freelancers have fallen into will help prevent you from making the same mistakes. I don't profess to be a model freelance journalist so here are some of my mistakes and suggested solutions.

Pitfall

Getting a commission and working on it exclusively and neglecting to look for the next piece of work.

Solution

This is a classic pitfall and can be avoided by taking Matthew Stibbe's advice of a 'pitch a day' (see Interview in Chapter 19). If you were completely overflowing with work, you could always store up the ideas in a notebook and save them for days when you are feeling slightly less inspired.

Pitfall

Having several pieces of work at the same time and working long hours to get them completed, to the detriment of the work.

Solution

Hitting a deadline is obviously vital but sleeping on a piece of work and looking at it again with fresh ideas is often time better spent than battling to stay awake through the night with the aid of ProPlus and Red Bull.

Pitfall

Neglecting 'boring' tasks like keeping invoices and spreadsheets up to date and then having to spend days sorting everything out in order to make a tax return.

Solution

Put aside an hour or so each week to complete admin.

Pitfall

You find yourself working for less money than you are happy with.

Solution

This is a tricky one and I realise that elsewhere I have suggested saying 'yes' to every job. Occasionally you will find that some people offer you work that just doesn't seem worth your while. You have to weigh up the pros and cons of this situation for yourself. One solution might be to negotiate with the client, using the methods recommended by Phil Sutcliffe in Chapter 21.

On the positive side, a poorly-paid job may lead to more work through contacts you make or you may be able to recycle the piece in the future. Plus, poor pay is better than no pay. Think through these possible advantages before you turn work away on the basis of it being a poor payer.

Planning

Plan your days, weeks and even your months. Planning a daily routine can prevent procrastination or being led astray. A daily routine might look something like this:

9–10	Daily pitch and idea generation
10–12	Writing commissioned piece
12–1	Updating accounts
1–2	Lunch
2–2.30	Interviewing for next article
2.30–4.30	More writing and filing piece
4.30–5.30	Researching next piece and discussion with editor

Over a week, plan time for speaking to contacts and colleagues.

Over a month you might need to plan some further training that you are undertaking, which in itself is planning for the future. Also factor in some networking events in the search for new stories.

Make lists

At the beginning of the week write a list of all the things you want to accomplish and keep returning to your list to make sure they are all done. If they don't get done, add them to the next week's list and so on until they are accomplished.

Tick off jobs as they are done – this will give you the sense that you are getting somewhere and moving forward. I also try not to make my lists too long for precisely this reason, and if I don't tick off everything on a day then I just roll it onto the next day. But don't avoid unpleasant tasks, as the longer you leave them the worse they seem to become.

Set goals

This is taking list-making to the next level; it is widely believed that setting goals increases the chances of you achieving them. Write down your goals and ambitions at the beginning of the year or month. I have done this on a few occasions and am often surprised that by focusing on an aspiration, such as the writing of this book, it does transpire.

■ Focus on your desire to achieve your goal.

■ Write your goal down.

■ Identify the obstacles that stand in your way and write them down in a list. These might be things like writing experience, confidence or further training.

■ Set a realistic deadline for achieving your goal. Be careful here, as missing a deadline can have a demotivating effect.

■ Make a concrete step-by-step plan for achieving your goal.

■ Visualise yourself completing your goal.

■ Prioritise the work and set about achieving your goal with perseverance and resolve. Don't give up – keep ploughing on even if it feels as though you aren't making headway.

■ Watch for small breakthroughs and congratulate yourself when you make them.

Don't procrastinate and stay motivated

Everyone has suffered with the desire to do something else other than what they should be doing. Without a boss breathing down your neck it can be tempting to do anything other than the task in hand. But as your own boss, you need to be able to have a word with yourself and get yourself motivated.

Check your bank balance every day – if a lack of funds going into your account doesn't motivate you, nothing will!

ORGANISATION

Use spreadsheets

You will need a spreadsheet for your accounts but also using a spreadsheet to keep an eye on how you spend your time could reveal a lot about your working methods and whether you are making the best use of your time.

That time is money is a well-worn cliché, but working freelance really makes this apparent. Unlike paid staff who, when the boss is out of the office, can spend an afternoon on Facebook and get paid for it, a freelancer can't. If you spend an afternoon not working hard, that means no money.

If you tot up the amount you are earning from each individual client, your spreadsheet can help you to work out who your best clients are. Record the hours that you spend working and from that calculate your hourly rate. For example:

You earn £475 from a national newspaper in a month.

This was for two pieces at £237.50 each.

Time spent was 30 hours (four days) which works out at £15.83 an hour.

Minus 22% for tax = £12.35 per hour.

This factors in all the time that you might have spent researching the story before you pitched it and all the other jobs that can eat up time.

If you really wanted to frighten yourself you could work out the equivalent annual salary of earning £15.83 an hour:

£585.71 based on a 37 hour week.

Minus four weeks holiday (unpaid of course) and one week sick leave (also unpaid) = £27,528.

Or £21,472 after tax.

Of course this is just a rough guide, but the payment rates for the articles are based on real rates that newspapers pay. This illustrates how important it is to be able to write quickly and reduce the time spent working on each piece.

TIME MANAGEMENT

Working flat out from 7 am until 7 pm isn't good time management. It is easy to think that putting in the hours is all that is required, but working smarter rather than harder is the key to making sure you don't burn yourself out and that you are still doing the job in years to come.

Tips for good time management

■ Plan the writing of pieces in the ways Brendan Foley suggests in Chapter 6. This really is designed to help you speed up the whole process and progress from writing a feature every week to a feature a day.

■ Keep on top of your accounts and submit your invoice once work is completed. That way you know exactly how much you are invoicing for but also how much you are receiving. This will prevent any last-minute panics when you realise there is no money in the bank.

■ Using the advice Matthew Stibbe offers in Chapter 19 of 'a pitch a day' should keep you with a steady supply of work.

■ Always hit your deadlines, as missing them might mean you aren't commissioned by that title again.

■ Even though you are 'free' as a freelancer, you will be more effective if you have set hours and have a designated place set aside to work.

Having said all this, there will be evenings spent working your fingers to the bone in order to hit a deadline. But the key is to be in control of your working life rather than it controlling you.

LIFE/WORK BALANCE

Enjoying your social life and learning to let go of work is essential for a freelancer. Many self-employed people have difficulty switching off and find themselves checking emails in the evenings or at weekends.

Remember the advice given in Chapter 11 on generating ideas and how important they are in the whole process of creating more work for yourself. Getting out and socialising with your friends or switching off from work and immersing yourself in something completely different will help you generate more ideas, relax and enjoy life. Perhaps most importantly, it will help you exercise the self-discipline that you need to enjoy freelancing and not become consumed by it. This is a real danger and could lead you to decide that freelancing isn't for you after all.

Interview: **Philippa Hobson, Creative & Cultural Skills**

Many issues that freelance journalists face are similar to those experienced by freelancers working in other creative and cultural sectors. Freelance journalists can therefore learn a lot from how others in the creative and cultural sectors go about their self-employed work.

Creative & Cultural Skills (www.ccskills.org.uk) is one of the few organisations that supports the activities of freelancers working in creative and cultural sectors. Creative & Cultural Skills adviser, Philippa Hobson, explains the organisation's role and how their work benefits freelancers.

What is the role of Creative & Cultural Skills?
Our role is to support people working in advertising, cultural heritage, music, crafts, design, performing, literary and visual arts. There are 265,000 self-employed people out of 678,480 in total working across the creative and cultural sector. These statistics derive from Creative & Cultural Skills' research.

What support do you offer exactly?

We provide information, advice and guidance to support career progression, improve skills or help break down barriers that prevent entry to the sector. For example, we have developed Creative Choices, the first online service to support every individual and business to get in, and get on in, the creative and cultural sector. We campaign for the sector; for example, making 'train to gain' accessible. We develop solutions that up skill the workforce such as developing our Cultural Leadership Programme, which runs specific training for freelancers.

We ensure qualifications meet employer needs. For example, with freelancers from across the sector we have written standards designed to help freelancers develop their skills and knowledge – for instance, how to write a risk plan or an export strategy. Our standard on risk planning identifies areas freelancers should be aware of, such as political and cultural changes or identifying new competitors in their areas of business.

We produce industry intelligence, recently publishing the Craft and Cultural Heritage Blueprints. These identify the specific needs of each sector. For example, in visual arts we have discovered that mid-career support is a big issue, so we will be working with other arts organisations to support people in this area. Our literature blueprint, which will be of interest to writers, is currently in development.

In your experience do freelancers have enough training?

This varies from sector to sector and from individual to individual. Freelancers working in visual arts fundraising for museums and galleries might have more structured training and development; for example, being supported by the Museums Association's accreditation programmes and the Institute of Fundraising's Continued Professional Development training.

Conversely an individual working in a studio as a craft practitioner might learn informally from the other crafts individuals. As part of our Creative Apprenticeship Programme, we are currently piloting a freelance music apprenticeship with Access to Music.

Are there similarities between freelancers across different sectors?

There are some common issues for freelancers that we have identified across sectors, such as the need to support the development of skills in areas such as marketing, communications and business.

Is freelancing becoming a more-favoured option throughout the creative industries?

In 2006–07 there were 101,600 freelancers in the creative and cultural industries and in 2008–09 there are 123,100 freelancers. This represents an increase of 21% in two years. In comparison, during the same period the creative and cultural industries experienced overall employment growth of only 9%.

Freelance work along with general self-employment and part-time work is generating this broader employment growth in the sector.

21

Negotiating

If you cast your mind back to a story's journey to publication (Chapter 12), you will remember that part of the process is the negotiation with an editor. As you will have gathered by now getting work is not an easy task, so when you do secure something it can be tempting just to accept whatever is put on the table.

Phil Sutcliffe is a music journalist and a tutor for the NUJ short training course 'Pitch and Deal'. In this chapter he shares his advice on how to negotiate successfully and why it is important to do so.

TIMING

It is at the point you have secured a commission and agreed what piece of work you are going to produce that you should ask about money. Phil suggests that to tee up the subject, you could either use a bit of humour by saying something like, 'So let's talk about money' or the more business-like, 'What is in the budget for this?'

'Many people hand power to the client here,' says Phil. 'But if you are selling, which we are, then the magic phrase is something like, "How much are you offering?"' The important thing is to put yourself in a position to ask for more. 'People are always scared of asking for more. Never be scared of this,' says Phil emphatically. 'In every class I have taken, I always ask if anyone has ever lost a job from doing this. And in ten years there has only been one.'

Freelancers very often find that the first offer isn't always the final offer. Plus there is actually a very high percentage of freelancers who manage to secure a better deal, sometimes this can be small and sometimes more significant. 'An experienced negotiator will keep bouncing back to you,' says Phil. But if you are aware of this, and realise that any improvement is better than if the subject hadn't been approached, then you shouldn't shy away from negotiating.

To give more backing to your claim, you could calculate how much you are going to need to charge for the piece, by working out how many hours it is likely to take.

ADDED PROFESSIONALISM

Once you have secured the best deal possible, Phil advises that you then put the most you can into your work. 'The tendency is for journalism to be de-professionalised at the moment,' he says, 'but value yourself and the skills that you can provide.' This will benefit everyone working in the industry.

Beyond money

Negotiation is a skill that is good to learn whatever kind of business you are in, and it is important to remember that, as a sole trader, you are in business.

Negotiation is important when you are agreeing what you will supply. For example, if it is suggested that you will provide photographs to accompany the piece, you should ask for a small fee to cover this extra work. Negotiating skills will also be useful when discussing elements of the story with the editor, what you are going to cover and what isn't going to be worth pursuing.

Further information

Pitch and Deal is a short course run by Phil Sutcliffe on behalf of the NUJ. Further details can be found here at www.nujtraining. org.uk

---

Interview: **John Toner, National Union of Journalists**

The National Union of Journalists (NUJ, www.nuj.org.uk) describe themselves as follows: 'We are an active, campaigning organisation seeking to improve the pay and conditions of our members and working to protect and promote media freedom, professionalism and ethical standards in all media.' John Toner deals specifically with the concerns of the Union's freelance members.

Why should freelancers join the NUJ?

Every freelance journalist needs an organisation that will provide support, and the NUJ is the best equipped to do that.

What support does the NUJ provide a freelance member?

The NUJ does many things:

- pursues non-payment of fees;
- provides advice on contracts and workers' rights;
- advises on copyright;
- issues the National Press Card;
- offers affordable training;
- arranges comprehensive and affordable professional indemnity insurance;
- assists in journalists getting work through the Freelance Directory;
- defends and supports press freedom;
- can be a lifeline through the International Federation of Journalists;
- enables communication with other journalists, both freelance and staff.

There are nearly 37,000 NUJ members. What percentage of them are freelance journalists?

Almost 25% of NUJ members are freelance.

What are the common day-to-day grievances from freelance journalists that you deal with?

Issues such as low rates, getting paid, protecting copyright and obtaining holiday pay are among the most common.

Are there larger issues facing freelancers?

Rates have stagnated over a long period; media companies also want more rights for the same rates. There are also the problems of police hindrance and access to cover events. These issues will face freelancers for many years to come.

Is there any evidence to suggest that the credit crunch has made things any better or worse for freelance journalists?
Over the past year, many companies have cut their freelance budgets. This means work either disappears or remains with reduced rates. With more freelancers competing for less work, things have become worse.

How much does it cost to join?
The standard fee is £15.75 per month, but no one need pay more than 1% of their income.

Is there any other advice you would offer someone thinking of becoming a freelance journalist?
A prospective freelancer should ask him/herself the following question: Can I handle the insecurity?

22

Self-employment checklist

REGISTER WITH INLAND REVENUE

The first thing to do is register yourself as a self-employed sole trader with the Inland Revenue:

Tel: 0845 915 4515

This is not as scary as it sounds. It is a simple phone call and then you can get on with some work and not worry about anything else for a while. Be warned though, that you must register within three months of going self-employed or risk a fine of £100.

PAYING TAX

You don't pay tax until you have submitted your first tax claim, which is done after your first year of trading. So you have a glorious 12 months of not paying tax and the temptation is to spend it all and worry about it later. I did this in my first year, and then wished I had saved the money in a separate account as people had advised me to do. Now I pay my tax monthly to keep on top of it. Oh well, you live and learn.

The easiest way to pay tax is to make a self-assessment claim and you do this by declaring how much profit you have made (see Keeping Accounts below). The Inland Revenue will then get back to you telling you how much tax you owe. If you have kept money for your tax obligations aside as you are advised to do, you can then pay it all immediately. If for some reason, like me, you are unable to pay it in full immediately, they may allow you to pay monthly. They are surprisingly reasonable.

These are the current levels of tax you can expect to pay in 2010:

- up to £6,985: 10%;

- standard rate on earnings between £6,766 and £37,295: 22%;

- basic rate on any income over £37,296: 40%.

Using an Accountant

If you are hopeless with figures, you might choose to use an accountant. An accountant can help you to make a claim, and a good one should be able to advise you on the expenses that you can claim against tax (travel or subscriptions, for example).

This extra, plus the amount of time it can save you, will often mean that employing an accountant will pay for itself. I like to work out how much money I am making as I go. This can help me make decisions based on what I am earning, such as this client is taking too long to pay or is not paying enough.

MAKING NATIONAL INSURANCE CONTRIBUTIONS

National Insurance (NI) contributions are separate from your tax and can be paid by monthly direct debit or by a quarterly bill. If you don't expect to make a great deal of money in your first year you can reduce your contributions.

Your pension may be affected if you don't make enough contributions, but they will allow you to make up payments at a later stage.

The National Insurance helpline number is 0845 915 4515.

SEPARATE BANK ACCOUNT

If an accountant does your tax return, they will prefer to check things off against your bank statements. In theory, this should be a business account but as you incur bank charges for business accounts many freelancers use current accounts and keep their personal finances in another account. Be aware that this requires a bit of juggling and transfers between banks take longer than transfers between accounts at the same bank.

KEEPING ACCOUNTS

There are two things your accounts need to record: what you spend and what you earn. The difference is your profit, and remember that you only pay tax on your profit. You need to keep a receipt for everything you spend. A tax inspector could ask at any time to see your accounts and they will want to see that everything is accounted for.

An Excel spreadsheet should be sufficient for most sole traders, but creating a spreadsheet does require a certain level of skill. Software packages like QuickBooks have a ready-made layout into which you can insert your incomings and outgoings.

CLAIMABLE EXPENSES

Capital allowances

In the first year of trading you can claim for capital allowances, which is the purchase of larger items essential for your work. In a journalist's case this includes equipment such as a dictaphone or a computer.

Travel

You can currently claim for 40p a mile, but only on journeys that you make for business.

Office costs

If you are working from home you can claim a proportion of your home bills. This is based on a percentage of a percentage. For example, if you turn your spare room into an office, what proportion of the house does that take up? A figure of 20% should be reasonable. Now, what percentage of time are you working there? Full-time? Great, claim the full amount. Part-time? Well, if you are working 2.5 days a week that is 50%.

I claim for a mobile phone and a small portion of my broadband bill. I also pay rent for some office space. So all of these expenses plus my monthly tax and NI contributions need to be covered before I start to make a profit.

OTHER CONSIDERATIONS

Keeping accurate records

The law requires you to keep records of all tax-related information. This includes bills, invoices you send and receive, bank statements and receipts for expenses. The more records you keep, the easier it will be when it comes to filing your tax return.

You must by law keep any records that relate to your business for a minimum of five years and ten months after the end of the tax year the records relate to. All of this is in case a tax inspector pays you a visit to check that your records are above board.

National Insurance

Class 2 NI contributions are currently at a flat rate of £2.40 a week (2009–10) if you earn over £5,075 per year. (This is your total earnings, not just from your self-employed work.) These contributions count towards your benefits, such as state pension, bereavement benefit and maternity leave. You can make these payments from a quarterly bill or by a monthly direct debit.

Class 2 NI contributions do not count towards jobseeker's allowance or statutory sick pay. You may wish to consider making other arrangements, such as a personal pension or income protection insurance.

If you earn less than £5,075 per year, by working part-time for example, you can apply for a certificate of small earnings exception and not pay Class 2 NI contributions. Bear in mind, however, that this could leave you vulnerable later should you need to claim the state benefits mentioned above.

Registering for VAT?

Registering for VAT (Value Added Tax) is necessary only if you supply goods and services with a value above £68,000. If this is the case, you can register on the Inland Revenue website or by phoning the Newly Self-employed Helpline on 0845 915 4515.

Tax deadlines

There are four key deadlines for sending in your tax return and paying your tax:

■ 31 October: paper tax return deadline.

■ 31 January: online tax return deadline.

■ 31 January: payment deadline for your bill from the previous tax year.

■ 31 July: deadline for your second payment on account, depending on your payment arrangements.

Further information: www.hmrc.gov.uk/selfemployed/

23

Self-employment: the pros and cons

Now that you have a good understanding of the process of how to become a freelance journalist, let's look at the realities of actually being one. If you are still trying to decide whether this is the career for you, consider the following pros and cons. I hope this exercise acts as a reality check so that you begin your career in freelance journalism with your eyes open.

PROS AND CONS OF BEING SELF-EMPLOYED

Going self-employed is actually a very easy step to take; it is the staying self-employed which is the tricky bit. And there is a whole host of pros and cons that you should think through before you take the leap.

As a self-employed person, you are no longer reliant on that belligerent boss who really only has his or her own interests at heart. However, the freedom you have on the one hand is tempered by the fact that you are more exposed to business risks. There is no protection between you and the forces of the marketplace; getting paid late is a classic example of this.

If you have a job and you have a bad day, oh well, we all have bad days at the office. Even on a bad day you still got paid, you still contributed to your pension and you could have taken a holiday day or a sick day. Life isn't so straightforward for the self-employed person. If I have a bad day and can't get anything done, I don't get paid until the piece of work is completed. And if I have a deadline and am sick, well the deadline still has to be met.

On the plus side, as I write, it is a glorious afternoon, so in theory I could go up to the park with the kids and enjoy the sunshine. If I put in a couple of hours tonight, then I will have satisfied my work quota for the week and can sleep happily in the knowledge that I am getting my job done.

Insecurity

Insecurity can come from many sources such as the lack of a regular wage and not having a manager to tell you what to do. There are also other elements that can come into play to stop you from ever getting too secure. Budgets may be changed, or run out. March is notoriously bad as many new budgets start at the beginning of April and you can find that editors have to be very tight in the final days of the year's budget.

There can be inexplicable droughts in work. Illness might take you out of the loop for a week or two and it might take you a week to get back on track, meaning that at the end of the month you realise you have only just made enough to pay the rent. August is another bad time when everyone disappears for a few weeks and automatic 'out of office' replies are the only responses to your emails. Christmas can be another disruption.

The only real way to deal with all of this is to forward plan, take the rough with the smooth and adopt a philosophical, 'water off a duck's back' kind of attitude.

Holidays

One my biggest headaches is taking a holiday. First of all I have to stop making pitches about two weeks before I go in the danger that I might get some work just before I leave. So in these last two weeks things quieten down; then I have the two blissful weeks off where I stop thinking about work. Then come the two weeks where I have to get things going again with a series of pitches, before getting completely overloaded with work again. So a holiday means six weeks disruption, then a frantic effort to claw back lost ground.

Ups and downs

So, the crux of being a self-employed freelancer is that it is a bit of a roller coaster. One month everyone pays on time, you have plenty of work, you are pleased with the variety of the work and the quality that you are providing. The next month can be a completely different story: nobody at all pays you, the bank is getting itchy, your landlord even itchier, you catch a cold and can't work for a few days (no sick pay), none of your ideas is accepted and that small bit of work you did have you managed to screw up taking twice as long as you should have. Funny how I found more examples on the negative side!

You can see that for some people this kind of existence isn't going to be what they are looking for. Although it is fair to say that not every freelancer will be like me: many have regular work with one or two clients and the fact they aren't actually staff is just a difference in paperwork. But these examples provide you with some food for thought if you are trapped in your day job, thinking that the grass looks greener on the other side. It isn't greener; it is just a different shade of green.

DEALING WITH THE INSECURITY

Be honest with yourself and check that you are prepared to face the following:

- fluctuating income;

- looking after your own administration including invoicing and tax returns;

- finding your own work;

- self-discipline of being your own boss;

- keeping yourself motivated;

- investing in your own training.

Having a mentor

Having someone you can discuss your work with can be very beneficial. This could be your partner but sometimes someone such as a mentor who has greater distance and can see things objectively is going to be the biggest help. Registering with local groups of small businesses can also be helpful for finding support and networking (see Chapter 19, Marketing Yourself).

An understanding partner

Taking a risk with your career and putting yourself in a position where your income is likely to fluctuate will inevitably affect those around you. If you are not the main breadwinner, you might have a little more financial freedom to take this risk. If you are single, you don't have anyone other than yourself to worry about. But if you are left waiting for a payment for a couple of months, you still might find yourself cap-in-hand at your parents' door or at the bank's door asking for a temporary loan. Think about contingency plans for worst-case scenarios before they happen, and then you will know what to do should the circumstance arrive.

Those around you will also need to know about the nature of the job and the strange and unusual ways it can make you behave. Facing deadlines inevitably causes stress and if you are working at home, this stress will be felt by others in the house. Talk to people whom you share your life with and explain to them what is going on.

PROS AND CONS OF BEING A FREELANCE JOURNALIST

You may have picked up as you've been reading this book that freelance journalism is a rewarding and inspiring way to make a living. Equally, you may have noticed that it is fraught with financial- and job-insecurity; great journalists leave or are being made to leave the profession every day through redundancy. I want to put this into perspective: for every great reason to become a journalist, there is just as valid an argument for finding a more sensible way to make a living and express yourself.

Pros	Cons
You have the keys to the city – call whoever you like and they will probably talk to you.	Nobody will really trust you once you say you are a journalist. Even if you tell them you aren't a tabloid journalist, you are still part of the sordid business that is the media.
You can start work tomorrow. As long as someone commissions you and is pleased with the work that you are providing, you can say you are a freelance journalist.	Just because you have done the work it doesn't necessarily mean you will get paid on time or at all. You might not get any more work from that publication if their budget runs out, or there may be other people willing to work for free.
You can fit your work around other commitments such as children, other work, etc.	An editor might call you and ask if you can turn a piece of work around in a few hours. If you say 'No', that might be the last you hear from them.

These are some of the realities of freelance journalism, as experienced by me and the countless other freelancers I have spoken to in researching this book. To further demonstrate how tough the mountain is to climb, consider the following.

The law of averages

By freelancing for a living the odds are stacked against you. This isn't just a dramatic line to grab your attention; it is also a statement of fact. Consider these statistical recollections.

In one class that I teach at Bath Spa University, students are encouraged to send over a term 18 pitches each, with a view to getting their work published. The average that students manage to achieve stands at around one commission per student. I'm sure you don't need me to tell you that this is a 1 in 18 ratio.

I remember moaning once to the editor of *The Big Issue* that I was getting only one in seven ideas accepted and I was surprised when he replied that he thought I was actually doing really well. He said that from his side of the fence he would probably commission one in every ten ideas sent in to him each day.

So let's take an average of one in ten ideas being accepted and imagine for a minute that the pay rate is decent, say £22 per 100 words, which is the *Guardian*'s rate. Now in an ideal world, for the freelancer to reach the UK's average rate of pay (currently £27,500) they would need to be making £479 a week. So that is two full-length pieces and one smaller piece. Three ideas commissioned based on the above ratio means that you will be pitching 30 ideas *per week*. Is this an impossible task? Nothing is impossible but it does put a few things into perspective.

This is based on working full-time and not allowing for any incoming commissions. Hopefully, as time goes by, you will be able to establish yourself and people will come to you looking for specific articles.

What I am trying to demonstrate is that ideas are an integral part of working as a journalist. You will need to have them in ample supply – a good working practice, as Matthew Stibbe suggests, is the 'pitch a day'. If nothing else, this will improve your pitching ability which will in turn improve your prospects of finding more work.

WHAT IS SUCCESS ANYWAY?

Your 'success', actually let's just say 'enjoyment of this profession', is often a case of how you react to these circumstances. All business involves an element of risk, and if you don't take risks, the chances are you will be unhappy anyway.

Susan Jeffers wrote a brilliantly-titled self-help book called *Feel the Fear and Do It Anyway*. The title alone has inspired me to push on and take risks when there has been a safer option available.

The other way to measure your success is to set your own personal goals and keep them in sight in order to achieve them (see Chapter 20, Planning, Organisation and Time Management for more on goal setting). If your goal is to be published in your favourite magazine and write about something that you are passionate about, that is fine. You don't have to make a full-time living as a freelance journalist to be able to call yourself one. There are many people working in this profession part-time and it seems that this is an increasing trend – probably because of some of the reasons given above!

But let's end on a good note and recall Brendan Foley's description of a freelance journalist as like being on 'a permanent Blue Peter special assignment but the price of the ticket is very high'.

24

Working from home

Working from home is an increasingly-popular choice with many benefits. It is ideal for people who have to juggle a family life around their work (see the interview with *Guardian* columnist Lia Leendertz in Chapter 8), people who want to lower their overheads, or those who just don't want to waste part of their day commuting with the rest of the rat race.

Although there are many benefits, there are also some drawbacks and in this chapter we will look at the pros and cons of working from home, some viable alternatives and also identify what you need to take into account should you decide that home working is for you.

Although many of us dream of not being stuck in an office, there are some things that you might miss. Forget about flirting with the HR manager, going out for a drink with work mates, having a crafty five minutes on Facebook, Christmas parties or any of the other delights of working in an office. Working freelance means that now there is just you. Does that sound ideal? Well, consider these points first.

ADVANTAGES

You're free

Nine to five? For losers. You can work wherever and whenever you want. Work from Starbucks if you like. Start at midday and knock off at 2 pm – if you can afford it!

You're the boss

Well done, you got the job. Your job is yours. You don't need to work your way up the ladder anymore, because there isn't one! You are your own boss.

Ditch the suit and tie

One of the great clichés about working from home is that you can work in your pyjamas. You could even work naked. Why not? Nobody can see you, except maybe your neighbours! All you need to do is to stagger into your spare room, or drag the laptop into your bed and cue the music, 'hi ho … hi hoooo'.

Portfolio working

'Flexible' is now your middle name and you may be asked to do all sorts of weird and wonderful things. Your job description could become harder to define, which is no bad thing really – in freelancing, every job can demand something slightly different.

I have been asked to talk to students about being a journalist, and to track down musicians for a music conference. With my PR hat on, I have worked at a food and wine festival and sold books overseas. Variety is the spice of life and doing 'other things' has got me out and about which in turn leads to more ideas and contacts for stories to pitch.

DISADVANTAGES

Working hours

You may be able to choose your hours in theory, but in reality there is an annoying hindrance in the fact that the rest of the world seems to work 9 to 5. So if you need to speak to someone for an interview, pitch something to an editor, chase the accounts payable department – in short, interact with the rest of the working world – it is going to have to be during business hours.

I hate to add insult to injury here, but statistics also show that self-employed people work some of the longest hours in the UK.

Cash flow

Being freelance means getting the work, doing the work (which could take a week) and then invoicing for it. Usual standard terms are payment within 30 days. I say 'usual' – it is also very usual that your clients might take a little longer. Then what are you going to do? Complain? Don't forget you want to get more work out of these people.

Cash flow is a perennial nightmare for any small-business person. Do the work, then weigh up whether you should do more work for that client. I have 'sacked' a couple of clients who were more hassle than they were worth. One way to do this is to calculate your hourly rate and then ask yourself if it was really worth it.

Self-discipline and self-management

One of the great things about not having a boss is that there is nobody there to check that you are doing your work properly, on time, on budget. Of course, clients will stop asking you to work for them if you miss deadlines but the point is that you are the one who has to get yourself up in the morning. Beware the temptation to roll over in bed and think 'I'll just have another 10 minutes', as that invariably means another hour.

Not having a manager means there is nobody to kick your butt, motivate you to get a job done and to say, 'Well done, you are doing a great job'. This is a very important point and it may be worth looking to see if you can find another freelance colleague to be a 'management buddy' for you to bounce ideas off. And to tell you that you are doing a great job but that you need to pull your finger out.

Hello? Is anybody there?

Remember Jack Nicholson in the film *The Shining*? In a snow-bound hotel in the middle of nowhere he busily types all day, every day. Only when the cabin fever has really set in and he starts running about the place with an axe in his hands do we see that all he has written, over and over again, is 'All work and no play makes Jack a dull boy'.

Working at home can give you cabin fever; not leaving the house, even for a breath of fresh air, can do funny things to the mind. I used to go for a ten-minute walk up to the park and back just to give myself a break between being at 'home' and 'work'. Otherwise you find yourself talking like a mad person at the first person who you have human contact with, which can be very embarrassing if it is the postman.

Family under your feet

The flip side of the loneliness and the isolation is not being able to concentrate or get things done because other people are getting under your feet. Family members or flatmates, the net result is the same – driving each other mad. As much as they are getting in your way, don't forget that you are also getting in their way. How would you like it if someone turned your home into an office? Not very homely is it?

The phone

If you are going to start using your home phone for business calls, do you really want your clients having to ask your kids if Mummy or Daddy is at home? It doesn't really create the right image of you as a professional.

CREATING A SEPARATE WORKSPACE

Having a separate working space is a necessity. Working at the kitchen table while the kids argue at breakfast or working in the TV room while your flatmate plays Nintendo, isn't going to be conducive to getting the job done.

In the interview in Chapter 8, Damian Barr explains how he works from a purpose-built shed in his garden. This is a great situation, keeping you close to the comforts of home but also providing the benefits of having your own space in which to think clearly. Whatever or wherever your separate space is, treat it like going to work and walk away from it at the end of your day. I mean this literally and metaphorically. This is good for you physically and mentally.

When setting up your workspace make it as professional as the space will allow and get yourself the following:

- wallplanner;
- diary;

- filing cabinet for all your invoices and accounts;

- magazine files;

- some stationery.

Also, make sure that your computer and desk are set up to health and safety standards. It is very easy to give yourself RSI by neglecting this and, importantly, if you have RSI, your ability to work will be inhibited. You can find advice about safe working practices on the HSE website (www.hse.gov.uk).

SHOULD I RENT AN OFFICE?

I rent an office for the following reasons:

- It gets me out of the house and this is good for me mentally.

- It is better for me physically as working from a laptop on my table in the spare room gives me backache. My rented office complies with all the health and safety regulations that I can't figure out at home.

- I rent a desk space on a monthly basis. This is a low commitment and I can leave with a month's notice should my work suddenly dry up.

- The cycle to and from my office keeps me fit and is good thinking time – I often get several ideas when I'm cycling.

- I meet people whom I wouldn't do normally. Remember that stories don't happen in isolation; the journalist needs to be around people and events that trigger ideas and relationships that lead to work.

■ I have found extra work by being part of a larger network. This is not always journalism but is often PR, which I welcome as it broadens my horizons and keeps me on my toes. Plus it saves me 'looking-for-work time', which in turn saves me money.

■ The office I work in belongs to a book publisher, so I have picked up a lot of knowledge about the book trade and I hope this will help me in the future.

■ Over time I have also developed a good relationship with the landlord and he understands if I can't pay the rent immediately because my cash flow is poor.

What you should consider before renting an office:

■ Will the financial outlay have a beneficial return? This doesn't always have to be an immediate financial return but could include being part of a wider network as I have mentioned above. In turn this will bring a financial benefit.

■ Is the office going to suit the kind of work you will be doing? If you will be making lots of phone calls and interviewing people by phone then perhaps somewhere busy where you wouldn't be disturbing colleagues would be appropriate.

■ Alternatively, is there a quiet space to go to within the office for a bit of peace?

■ Are you committed long term, or can you leave if things don't work out?

■ Is the location good? An industrial estate on the edge of town might be cheap but is it convenient if you need to meet a client in town for a coffee?

Appendix 1

Jargon buster

Angle

What approach is the article taking – is it a critical review or a trashing in the form of an opinion piece?

Anchor

A small feature that sits at the bottom of a page. It can be quirky or unusual.

Byline

Literally the part of the article that says 'by Marc Leverton'. If it is not included in the published version, you might hear a journalist say, 'Where's my byline?' This is because you can't really add it to your portfolio if it doesn't have your name on it.

Caption

Freelancers often source photos for articles and you may be asked who is in a picture or what is going on in it, so that the editor can drum up a caption.

Copy

A term for words that fill a page. 'I need more copy for this page. Can you knock me up a 200-word anchor piece?'

Deadline day
When the shit hits the fan.

Diary
Newspapers with lots of journalists and photographers covering different things in a city need to be co-ordinated. As in, 'Is this in the diary?'

Doorstepping
Horrible invasive technique used by tabloid journalists and paparazzi. Don't do it. Hacks camp outside someone's residence until they come out, where upon the victim is ambushed with a barrage of questions. This can last for as long as that person is deemed 'newsworthy'.

Filler
Similar to a NiB (see page 204) but fitting around another story.

Flannel panel
The little box or column found in a magazine that identifies the people involved in its production. An aspiring journalist can look for phone numbers and email addresses of staff here before making their pitch.

Gonzo Journalism
Made famous in the 1970s by US journalist Hunter S. Thompson. It has a punchy style and disregards many of the conventional rules of journalism. Also see New Journalism.

Headlines
Story headings for which, due to lack of space, words are dropped to create a strange language of their own, sometimes referred to as 'Headlinese'. For example, a headline to describe the unexpected sacking of a disc jockey might read 'Shock Jock's shock drop' which wouldn't really make much sense in any other context.

Hook

Is the hook strong enough? 'This needs a stronger hook' is something you might hear amid another rejection. The hook is the part of your story that makes it relevant to be written about at that specific time. So editors might want to publish a story about adoption during Adoption Week or write about college courses at the beginning of September.

In the gutter

The 'gutter' refers to a printed publication's central fold so if your story is positioned close to the fold this isn't such an ideal spot as, say, an outside right-hand page. If you think about how your eyes flow through a magazine, many people look only at the right-hand side of a page if they're just flicking through. In advertising the right-hand page can be sold for more revenue for precisely this reason.

Journalese

An Orwellian-sounding expression for the times when journalists forget they are speaking to normal people who have no idea what they are talking about.

Lead

A 'lead story' is the first one in a paper. It is given the highest priority, as it will be the focus of the most amount of attention.

New Journalism

Like Hunter S. Thompson's Gonzo Journalism, this style of journalism marked a change to traditional journalism rules. The term was coined by Tom Wolfe in 1970s USA. He attempted to bring a more fictional style of writing to journalism and aimed to 'get in the head' of the subject he was writing about.

Newswires
Stories sent out by press agencies from around the world

NiB
A 'News in Brief' column that runs down the side of a page. Each piece is no longer than a couple of sentences or a paragraph.

Paparazzi
Photographers who take unsolicited photos of celebrities for the tabloids. The term was coined in Italy and is the plural of 'paparazzo', which means 'mosquito'.

Photojournalism
Invited photographers who take photos at the request of an editor. These can be posed for individual features or larger events such as press conferences.

Pointer
Final line in a news item that entices the reader to come back for an update on a story. The classic example being, 'The case continues next week'.

Press conference
The assembly of members of the press to hear the announcement of something newsworthy; for example, an announcement by a government department.

PRs
A PR is the public relations person – a journalist's friend, source of stories and pain in the neck. The same term is applied to press officers and communications officers. It is not to be confused with the 'press release' which is the PR's tool.

Press release

A page or two of information that should be of interest to the press and contain a potential story. Journalists are inundated with press releases, which are usually sent by email (or fax, post or carrier pigeon), often blocking inboxes to the extent where your pitch emails can't be found. Journalists have been accused of just regurgitating press releases, a process that journalist Nick Davies, author of *Flat Earth News*, calls 'churnalism'.

Print-ready PDFs

Once the publication's designer has laid out the page including your story, they might send you a copy for your portfolio or perhaps to proof yourself before it goes to press.

Pull quote

Quotes that are designed to draw a reader into a story, but that also act to break up great swathes of text which may be unappealing for a reader. They tend to be strong or emotional quotes that relate directly to the story. The text is enlarged sufficiently to make it easy to spot on the page, and positioned to catch the eye of the reader who is flicking through the publication.

Readership

The audience of the newspaper or magazine.

Scoop

Being the first to report on a story, which is often then jumped on by other media after it has made print.

Shorthand

Abbreviated style of writing which saves journalists time, and captures quotes without the need to transcribe recordings.

Appendix 2

Further reading

USEFUL WEBSITES

www.nuj.co.uk
Website of the NUJ (National Union of Journalists), offering lots of invaluable information on journalism.

www.journalism.co.uk
A very good job listings section, which includes work experience and intern requests.

www.pressgazette.co.uk
Journalism trade magazine with jobs.

www.holdthefrontpage.co.uk
A more newspaper-focused website that has industry news and job listings.

www.ppa.co.uk
Website of the PPA (Periodical Publishers Association), which contains magazine industry information and updates. This reputable organisation is behind the annual PPA awards and they also offer training courses. Their website includes a database of all

their members – great for providing inspiration in response to the question, 'Who am I going to write for next?'

www.mediauk.com
A searchable database of all UK-based media. For example, search for 'Swansea' and see what media companies are based there.

www.londonfreelance.org/ratesforthejob
Part of the NUJ, on which freelancers have posted the payment they have received from media organisations for certain types of articles. Includes shift rates, rates per 100 words and other titbits such as 'had to haggle' or 'waited 3 months for payment'. Not comprehensive but strangely entertaining.

www.contractorcalculator.co.uk
Very informative website that includes online calculators for working out your after tax earnings, as well as other jiggery pokery like being able to work out your annual income by putting in an hourly rate.

WRITING AND EDITORIAL GUIDANCE

www.Badlanguage.net
Matthew Stibbe's blog offering writing tips.

www.realfoodlover.wordpress.com/winklers-writing-rules
Food writer Elizabeth Winkler gives her writing tips.

Editorial guidelines

www.bbc.co.uk/guidelines/editorialguidelines/advice/
www.guardian.co.uk/guardian/article/0,,180763,00.html

Style guides

www.guardian.co.uk/styleguide
www.timesonline.co.uk/tol/tools_and_services/specials/style_
guide

BOOKS

The Freelance Writer's Handbook by Andrew Crofts (Piatkus)
ISBN: 978-0749927639

About freelance writing generally, not specifically journalism.
The Writer's Handbook edited by Barry Turner (Macmillan)
ISBN: 978-0230573239
Updated every year but any recent year should suit you to begin
with. Contains a good list of magazine contacts.

Flat Earth News by Nick Davies (Vintage)
ISBN: 978-0099512684
Great for understanding the process which Davies calls
'churnalism' and inspiring journalists to avoid it.

MAGAZINE PUBLISHING HOUSES

Dennis Publishing
Set up by the legendary publisher Felix Dennis, who was a
founder of the counter culture magazine *Oz* in the 1960s. Today
they publish 18 titles such as *Mac User*, *Auto Express*, *Computer
Shopper*, *Custom PC*, *PC Pro*, *Viz*, *Fortean Times*, *Poker Player*, *Monkey*,
Bizarre, *The Week* and *Total Gambler*. www.dennis.co.uk

Haymarket

Haymarket Media Group is the UK's largest privately-owned publishing company. They publish many business titles including *Brand Republic*, *Campaign*, *Management Today* and *Media Week*. Their list of consumer titles features *FourFourTwo*, *Stuff* and *What Hi-Fi?* amongst many others. www.haymarket.com

Future Publishing

Future are based in Bath and London and produce more than 80 specialist titles based around technology, cars, cycling, film and photography. Well known titles include *Classic Rock*, *Total Film*, *Metal Hammer* and *SFX* magazines. www.futureplc.com

Appendix 3

Further training

If this book has whetted your appetite but you would like to get more formal training before heading into the media jungle, here is a list of journalism training providers across the UK.

JOURNALISM TRAINING PROVIDERS

National Council for the Training of Journalists (NCTJ)
NCTJ accredit a great deal of the journalism-training schemes in the UK. They also provide careers information, distance learning, short courses and continuing professional development, information and research, publications and events.

NCTJ Training Ltd
The New Granary, Station Road, Newport, Saffron Walden
Essex CB11 3PL
Tel: 01799 544014
E-mail: info@nctj.com
Website: www.nctj.com

NUJ Training
A resource for all journalists, whether established or new entrants, who are interested in taking the next step in their careers.

NUJ
308–312 Gray's Inn Rd
London WC1X 8D
Tel: 0207 278 7916
E-mail: info@nuj.org.uk
Website: www.nujtraining.org.uk

The following list provides details of colleges and universities running courses in journalism and related fields in the UK. Courses with accreditation from the National Council for the Training of Journalists (NCTJ), the Broadcast Journalism Training Council (BJTC) and/or the Periodicals Training Council (PTC) are noted.

This list is reproduced by kind permission of The MediaWise Trust (www.mediawise.org.uk), a registered charity based at the University of the West of England (UWE) providing advice, information, research and training on media ethics.

Bell College of Technology (BJTC)
Almada St, Hamilton
Lanarkshire ML3 OJB
Tel: 01698 283 100
E-mail: k.scott@bell.ac.uk
Website: www.bell.ac.uk

Birmingham City University (BJTC)
Department of Media & Communication, Perry Barr
Birmingham B42 2SU
Tel: 0121 331 5719
E-mail: media@bcu.ac.uk
Website: www.mediacourses.com

Bournemouth University (NCTJ, BJTC, PTC)
Bournemouth Media School, Fern Barrow, Poole
Dorset BH12 5BB
Tel: 01202 965 360
E-mail: media@bournemouth.ac.uk
Website: www.media.bournemouth.ac.uk

Cardiff University (NCTJ, BJTC, PTC)
Centre for Journalism Studies, Bute Building
King Edward VII Avenue
Cardiff CF31 3NB
Tel: 029 2087 4041
E-mail: HarrisRL@cardiff.ac.uk
Website: www.cardiff.ac.uk/jomec

Cardonald College (NCTJ)
690 Mosspark Drive
Glasgow G52 3AY
Tel: 0141 272 3242
E-mail: cmss@cardonald.ac.uk
Website: www.cardonald.ac.uk

City College of Brighton & Hove (NCTJ)
The Brighton Centre for Journalism, 11–14 Kensington Street
Brighton BN1 4AJ
Tel: 01273 684684
E-mail: journalism@ccb.ac.uk
Website: www.ccb.ac.uk

City University (BJTC, PTC)
Department of Journalism, Northampton Square
London EC1V 0HB
Tel: 020 7040 5060
E-mail: journalism@city.ac.uk
Website: www.city.ac.uk/journalism

Clarendon City College
New College Nottingham, Adams Building Centre, Stoney Street
The Lace Market Nottingham NG1 1LJ
Tel: 0115 910 4502
E-mail: andy.harrison@ncn.ac.uk
Website: www.ncn.ac.uk

Coleg Gwent (NCTJ)
Headquarters, The Rhadyr
Usk NP15 1XJ
Tel: 01495 333 333
E-mail: info@coleggwent.ac.uk
Website: www.coleggwent.ac.uk

Cornwall College (NCTJ)
Trevenson Road, Pool, Redruth
Cornwall TR15 3RD
Tel: 01209 616 161
E-mail: t.beattie@cornwall.ac.uk
Website: www.cornwall.ac.uk

Crawley College (NCTJ)
College Road, Crawley
West Sussex RH10 1NR
Tel: 01293 442 200
E-mail: information@crawley-college.ac.uk
Website: www.crawley-college.ac.uk

Cumbria Institute of the Arts (NCTJ)
Brampton Road, Carlisle
Cumbria CA3 9AY
Tel: 01228 400 300
E-mail: jackie.errigo@cumbria.ac.uk
Website: www.cumbria.ac.uk

Darlington College (NCTJ)
Cleveland Avenue, Darlington
County Durham DL3 7BB
Tel: 01325 503 030
E-mail: tmetcalf@darlington.ac.uk
Website: www.darlington.ac.uk

De Montfort University (NCTJ)
The Gateway
Leicester LE1 9BH
Tel: 0116 255 1551
E-mail: tosulliv@dmu.ac.uk
Website: www.dmu.ac.uk

East Surrey College (NCTJ)
Gatton Point, Claremont Road, Redhill
Surrey RH1 2JX
Tel: 01737 772 611
E-mail: studentservices@esc.ac.uk
Website: www.esc.org.uk

Edge Hill College (NCTJ)
St Helens Road, Ormskirk
Lancashire L39 4QP
Tel: 01695 575 171
E-mail: poolec@edgehill.ac.uk
Website: www.edgehill.ac.uk

Falmouth College of Arts (BJTC)
Woodlane Campus, Falmouth
Cornwall TR11 4RH
Tel: 01326 211 077
E-mail: denis@falmouth.ac.uk
Website: www.falmouth.ac.uk

Glasgow Caledonian University
Division of Media Culture and Leisure Management,
70 Cowcaddens Road
Glasgow G4 0BA
Tel: 0141 331 3000
E-mail: dmcg@gcal.ac.uk
Website: www.gcal.ac.uk

Goldsmiths College (BJTC)
University of London, New Cross
London, SE14 6NW
Tel: 020 7919 7171
E-mail: media-comms@gold.ac.uk
Website: www.goldsmiths.ac.uk/departments/media-
communications

Harlow College (NCTJ)
Velizy Avenue, Town Centre, Harlow
Essex CM20 3LH
Tel: 01279 868 000
E-mail: learninglink@harlow-college.ac.uk
Website: www.harlow-college.ac.uk

Harrow College (NCTJ)
Lowlands Road, Harrow
Middlesex HA1 3AQ
Tel: 0208 909 6000
E-mail: enquiries@harrow.ac.uk
Website: www.harrow.ac.uk/website/home.html

Highbury College, Portsmouth (NCTJ, BJTC, PTC)
School of Media & Journalism, Dovercourt Road, Cosham
Portsmouth
Hampshire PO6 2SA
Tel: 023 9238 3131
E-mail: glenne.martin@highbury.ac.uk
Website: www.highbury.ac.uk

Lambeth College (NCTJ)
Vauxhall Centre, Belmore Street, Wandsworth
London SW8 2JY
Tel: 020 7501 5010
E-mail: dnoble@lambethcollege.ac.uk
Website: www.lambethcollege.ac.uk

Liverpool Community College (NCTJ)
Journalism School, The Arts Centre, 9 Myrtle Street
Liverpool L7 7JA
Tel: 0151 707 8528
E-mail: angela.birchall@liv-coll.ac.uk
Website: www.liv-coll.ac.uk

London College of Printing (BJTC, PTC)
School of Media, 10 Back Hill
London EC1 5EN
Tel: 020 7514 6500
E-mail: r.f.l.smith@lcp.linst.ac.uk
Website: www.lcp.linst.ac.uk

Napier University
School of Communication Arts, Craighouse Campus
Craighouse Road
Edinburgh EH10 5LG
Tel: 0131 455 6150
E-mail: r.melville@napier.ac.uk
Website: www.napier.ac.uk

North West Regional College (NCTJ)
Derry City, Strand Rd
Londonderry BT48 7AL
Tel: 028 7127 6000
E-mail: ciaran.brolly@nwrc.ac.uk
Website: www.nwrc.ac.uk

Nottingham Trent University (BJTC)
Centre for Broadcasting & Journalism, Burton Street
Nottingham NG1 4BU
Tel: 0115 848 5803
E-mail: cbj@ntu.ac.uk
Website: www.cbj.ntu.ac.uk

St Mary's College
School of Communication, Culture & Creative Arts
Waldegrave Road
Twickenham TW1 4SX
Tel: 020 8240 4008
E-mail: minogued@smuc.ac.uk
Website: www.smuc.ac.uk/ccca

Sheffield College (NCTJ)
Norton Centre, Dyche Lane
Sheffield S8 8BR
Tel: 0114 260 3603
E-mail: mail@sheffcol.ac.uk
Website: www.sheffcol.ac.uk

Sheffield Hallam University (BJTC)
School of Cultural Studies, Psalter Lane Campus
Sheffield S11 8UZ
Tel: 0114 225 2607
E-mail: cultural@shu.ac.uk
Website: www.shu.ac.uk/schools/cs/

South East Essex College (NCTJ)
Carnarvon Road, Southend-On-Sea
Essex SS2 6LS
Tel: 01702 220 400
E-mail: syd.moore@southend.ac.uk
Website: www.se-essex-college.ac.uk

Southampton Institute (NCTJ, PTC)
East Park Terrace
Southampton S014 OYN
Tel: 023 80319653
E-mail: David.Berry@solent.ac.uk
Website: www.solent.ac.uk

Staffordshire University (NCTJ, BJTC)
Department of Journalism, School of Humanities & Social
Sciences, Staffordshire University
Stoke-on-Trent ST4 2DE
Tel: 01782 294415
E-mail: m.temple@staffs.ac.uk
Website: www.staffs.ac.uk

Surrey Institute of Art & Design (BJTC, PTC)
University College, Farnham Campus, Falkner Road, Farnham
Surrey GU9 7DS
Tel: 01252 722 441
E-mail: mconboy@surrart.ac.uk
Website: www.surrart.ac.uk/index2.html

Sutton Coldfield College (NCTJ)
Lichfield Road
Sutton Coldfield B74 2NW
Tel: 0121 355 5671
E-mail: cedwards@sutcol.ac.uk
Website: www.sutcol.ac.uk

Trinity and All Saints College (NCTJ, BJTC)
Centre for Journalism, Brownberrie Lane, Horsforth
Leeds LS18 5HD
Tel: 0113 283 7100
E-mail: m_hampton@tasc.ac.uk
Website: www.tasc.ac.uk

University College Chester (NCTJ)
Media Department, University College Chester, Binks Building
Parkgate Road
Chester CH1 4BJ
Tel: 01244 392 715
E-mail: w.johnstone@chester.ac.uk
Website: www.chester.ac.uk

University of Brighton (NCTJ)
Chelsea School, Hillbrow, Denton Road, Eastbourne
East Sussex BN20 7SR
Tel: 01273 643 703
E-mail: m.green@brighton.ac.uk
Website: www.brighton.ac.uk

University of Central Lancashire (NCTJ, BJTC)
Department of Journalism, Preston
Lancashire PR1 2HE
Tel: 01772 894730
E-mail: meward@uclan.ac.uk
Website: www.ukjournalism.org

University of Glasgow (NCTJ)
1 The Square
Glasgow G12 8QQ
Tel: 0141 330 4575
E-mail: S.Procter@admin.gla.ac.uk
Website: www.gla.ac.uk

University of Leeds (BJTC)
The Institute of Communications Studies
Leeds LS2 9JT
Tel: 0113 343 5800
E-mail: robin@ics-server.novell.leeds.ac.uk
Website: www.leeds.ac.uk/ics

University of Lincoln
Lincoln School of Journalism, Brayford Pool
Lincoln LN6 7TS
Tel: 01522 882 000
E-mail: jtulloch@lincoln.ac.uk
Website: www.lincoln.ac.uk/journalism

University of Sheffield (NCTJ, BJTC)
Department of Journalism Studies, 171 Northumberland Road
Sheffield S10 1DF
Tel: 0114 222 5000
E-mail: journalism@sheffield.ac.uk
Website: www.shef.ac.uk/journalism

University of Stirling
Department of Film and Media Studies
Stirling FK9 4LA
Tel: 01786 467 520
E-mail: j.m.mckay@stir.ac.uk
Website: www.fms.stir.ac.uk/index.html

University of Strathclyde (NCTJ)
Scottish Centre for Journalism Studies, Crawfurd Building
Jordanhill Campus, 76 Southbrae Drive
Glasgow G13 1PP
Tel: 0141 950 3281
E-mail: gordon.j.smith@strath.ac.uk
Website: www.strath.ac.uk

University of Ulster (NCTJ)
Cromore Road, Coleraine,
Co. Londonderry BT52 1SA
Tel: 08700 400 700
E-mail: online@ulst.ac.uk
Website: www.ulster.ac.uk
University of Wales College, Newport
Caerleon Campus, PO Box 101, Newport
South Wales NP18 3YH
Tel: 01633 432 432
E-mail: uic@newport.ac.uk
Website: www.rtschool.newport.ac.uk/welcome.html

University of the West of England
School of Creative Arts, St Matthias Campus
Oldbury Court Road
Bristol BS16 2JP
Tel: 0117 32 84591
E-mail: sca.enquiries@uwe.ac.uk
Website: www.uwe.ac.uk/sca

University of Westminster (BJTC, PTC)
Dept. of Journalism and Mass Communication, Harrow Campus
Watford Road, Northwick Park, Harrow
Middlesex HA1 3TP
Tel: 0207 911 5903
E-mail: Paddy.Scannell@wmin.ac.uk
Website: www.wmin.ac.uk

University of Wolverhampton (BJTC)
School of Humanities, Languages and Social Sciences
Millennium City Building, Stafford Street
Wolverhampton WV1 1SB
Tel: 01902 323518
E-mail: D.Foy@wlv.ac.uk
Website: www.wlv.ac.uk/Default.aspx?page=6968

Warwickshire College (NCTJ)
Warwick New Road, Leamington Spa
Warwickshire CV32 5JE
Tel: 01926 318 000
E-mail: enquiries@warkscol.ac.uk
Website: www.warkscol.ac.uk

Wolverhampton College (NCTJ)
Wulfrun Campus, Paget Road
Wolverhampton WV6 0DU
Tel: 01902 836 000
E-mail: mail@wolverhamptoncollege.ac.uk
Website: www.wolverhamptoncollege.ac.uk

BURSARIES FOR JOURNALISM TRAINING

Journalism Diversity Fund
This fund has been set up by those in the industry who want to join together to support the training of journalists from ethnically and socially diverse backgrounds.
www.journalismdiversityfund.com

The Scott Trust

The Scott Trust owns the *Guardian*. Their foundation also funds ten internships and bursaries for aspiring journalists each year. www.gmgplc.co.uk/scotttrust

Index